W9-BSQ-868

Pooled Data for Financial Markets

by
Terry E. Dielman

UNIVERSITY LIBRARY
GOVERNORS STATE UNIVERSITY
PARK FOREST SOUTH, ILL.

WITHDRAWN

umi
RESEARCH PRESS

Copyright © 1980, 1979
Terry Edward Dielman
All rights reserved

Produced and distributed by
UMI Research Press
an imprint of
University Microfilms International
Ann Arbor, Michigan 48106

Library of Congress Cataloging in Publication Data

Dielman, Terry E   1952-
   Pooled data for financial markets.

   (Research for business decisions ; no. 31)
   Bibliography: p.
   Includes index.
   1. Stock price forecasting—Statistical methods. 2. Time
series analysis.   I. Title. II. Series.

HG4636.D53 1980   332.63'222   80-22508
ISBN 0-8357-1130-7

HG
4636
.D53
1980

Contents

UNIVERSITY LIBRARY
GOVERNORS STATE UNIVERSITY
PARK FOREST SOUTH, ILL.

Figures

Tables

Abbreviations

RCR	Random Coefficient Regression
SUR	Seemingly Unrelated Regression
OLS	Ordinary Least Squares
GLS	Generalized Least Squares
LR	Likelihood Ratio
ML	Maximum Likelihood
ANOVA	Analysis of Variance
ANCOVA	Analysis of Covariance
LSDV	Least Squares with Dummy Variables
MSE	Mean Squared Error
MVLU	Minimum Variance Linear Unbiased
CRSP	Center for Research on Security Prices
NBER	National Bureau of Economic Research

Acknowledgments

I would like to thank Dr. Roger Wright, Dr. Timothy Nantell, Dr. William Wrobleski and Dr. E. Phillip Howrey for their valuable assistance in completing this study. Thanks also go to Dr. W. Allen Spivey, whose comments and suggestions on my proposal were most helpful.

Chapter 1

Introduction and Overview

Large data bases consisting of observations over time on a number of variables for many individuals (households, firms, countries, etc, individuals referred to as cross-sectional units) present a considerable problem for the researcher interested in a coherent analysis. As always, some type of structure must be imposed in order for any reasonable analysis to be done. This research is concerned with relationships believed to be linear but non-deterministic for each individual. The simplest form of such a relationship for individual i can be written as

$$y_{it} = a_i + b_i X_{it} + e_{it} \qquad (1.1)$$

where we believe y, the dependent variable, is linearly related to X, the independent or explanatory variable. The coefficient, b_i, represents the change in the dependent variable with respect to a change of one unit in the independent variable. The term e_{it} is a random variable, thus adding the non-deterministic nature to an otherwise exact relationship.

In this research we consider the case where we have a number of such relationships, say N, corresponding to N individual units; the model is also extended to more than one explanatory variable. We can now question whether each individual, i, should be analyzed as a separate entity or whether the group of individuals should be analyzed as a whole (pooling the time series and cross-sectional data). We must also determine appropriate methods to use in such analyses. These questions are addressed in subsequent chapters.

Special attention is given to the case where our N individuals constitute a sample from some larger population. The desire for inferences concerning characteristics of the population is an important factor in determining an appropriate method for analyzing the data.

Throughout much of this study a specific financial example is used as a vehicle for discourse. This should not be interpreted as an implication that the models discussed or that the study in general will be useful only to researchers in the field of finance. The methods should be widely applicable in any field where an analysis of pooled data is to be performed.

One intention of this study is to provide guidelines for researchers with limited statistical expertise who are faced with the task of analyzing pooled cross-sectional and time series data. As will be noted, certain chapters have been designed specifically for this purpose.

Another contribution is made in the development of hypothesis testing procedures for use with certain of the models. These results are technical in nature and will be of interest to researchers with a fair degree of mathematical training.

Finally, a contribution is made in the field of finance through an analysis of financial market data. It should be pointed out that this research does not intend to advance the theoretical boundaries of capital market theory. Capital market theory will be discussed when necessary but my contribution in finance will be empirical rather than theoretical.

The remainder of Chapter 1 summarizes work in each chapter and appendix of the study. Contributions in each chapter are noted. Since the interests of readers will vary, the summary is presented in three separate sections. Each section is designed to guide readers with specific interests to the chapters that will be most useful to them.

Section 1.1   Guidelines for Empirical Research

The researcher interested in performing an analysis of pooled data while avoiding any extensive mathematical development of the techniques is directed to Chapters 2 and 5.

In Chapter 2, models appropriate for use under various sets of assumptions are summarized and the literature is reviewed. References are cited for articles which discuss technical details and small sample properties, and for articles which apply the techniques in analysis of data. Appendix B summarizes studies of small sample properties for certain of the models discussed.

The presentation in Chapter 2 is placed in the context of an analysis of financial market data to facilitate reading by the empirical analyst and to provide examples. The reader with applications in a field other than finance may wish to omit Sections 2.2 and 2.3.

In Chapter 5 an outline or schema intended to guide the researcher in structuring an analysis of pooled data is presented. A model is chosen by considering the hypotheses formulated by the researcher, the assumptions the researcher is willing to make and the results of statistical tests of hypotheses. Various hypothesis testing procedures developed in Chapters 3 and 4 are summarized and several previously developed tests for determining model specification are discussed.

The schema is presented in three sections:

Section 5.1 Model Selection
Section 5.2 Testing of Assumptions (about residuals)
Section 5.3 Variable Choice

References are provided for additional reading in each of the three sections.

Section 1.2 Analysis of Financial Market Data

The empirical analysis performed in Chapter 6 provides information on the behavior of stock rate of return and systematic risk in months around the date of a stock repurchase announcement. The methodology used provides certain information concerning this behavior that was not available in previous analyses. The analysis also serves as an illustration of the schema presented in Chapter 5 and as an example of the use of many of the techniques developed in previous chapters.

An appendix to the analysis is included which may also interest the finance reader. Appendix E contains a graphical presentation of many of the Chapter 6 results and some descriptive statistics.

Although Chapter 6 can be understood without reference to other chapters, the reader interested in the analysis of stock market data may want to begin with the reading in Appendix A and that suggested in Section 1.1. Reading Appendix A and Chapters 2 and 5 in their entirety will solidify the methodological foundation of the reader and provide much insight into the reasoning behind the choice of methodology.

Section 1.3 Random Coefficient Regression Developments

For the reader with specific interests in the random coefficient regression (RCR) model or the mixed RCR model and with a fairly strong mathematical and statistical background, the following reading is suggested:

Appendix C presents a fairly rigorous mathematical representation of the mixed RCR model. A double purpose is served by starting with this appendix since notation and terminology used throughout the study are precisely defined, and since previously developed results are discussed.

Chapter 3 extends hypothesis testing pocedures for the mixed RCR model to include the following:

1. A test for randomness for a subset of the random coefficients.

2. A test for mean equal zero for a subset of coefficient means (or fixed coefficients).

3. A simultaneous test of randomness and mean equal zero for any subset of random coefficients.

Two alternative tests for randomness are compared by a small scale simulation in Appendix D. The results are included in Chapter 3.

Also discussed in detail in Chapter 3 is the problem of negative variance estimates, which are not an uncommon occurrence when using the RCR model. The effect of these negative variance estimates on t-statistics is examined and implications of the results for hypothesis testing procedures used with the RCR model are noted.

In Chapter 4, tests of assumptions about residuals are discussed and two tests are developed:

1. A test of the hypothesis that no serial correlation exists in any of the N individual time series.

2. A test of the hypothesis that no contemporaneous correlation exists.

These tests may be applied with several of the models for pooled data besides the RCR model as will be noted. The tests are specifically designed for use with pooled cross-sectional and the time series data and, as such, were not previously available.

In summary, we note that the intent of this study is threefold:

1. To provide guidelines for analyzing pooled data that can be easily understood by empirical researchers.

2. To analyze the effects of stock repurchase announcements on stock return characteristics by applying pooling methodology.

3. To develop tests of hypothesis useful in determining appropriate specification in models of pooled data.

Chapter 2

Analyzing Financial Market Data

Section 2.1 Introduction

Chapter 2 is a summary of the models useful in the analysis of data appearing as times series observations for many individual (cross-sectional) units. It is directed at those readers whose interest is in performing such an analysis rather than understanding the mathematics involved. Thus, the technical aspects of estimation and inference in the models is omitted (although references are included for the interested reader).

Throughout this chapter a financial example is used as a vehicle for discourse. The models presented in Section 2.4 have general applicability, however. Readers strictly interested in methodology for analyzing pooled data may want to begin with this section and forego the discussion of the financial analysis in the preceding sections. Section 2.4 examines the following models useful in the analysis of pooled cross-sectional and time series data:

1. The Extremes
    A. Separate Time Series Regressions and Seemingly Unrelated Regressions
    B. Classical Pooling
    C. Aggregation of Individual Relationships
2. The Covariance or Dummy Variable Model
3. The Error Components Model
4. The Random Coefficient Regression (RCR) Model
5. The Mixed RCR Model

Again, it should be emphasized that the financial example used throughout this chapter is included to facilitate reading and is not intended to discourage those readers whose applications lie in other fields. The reader interested in a more detailed mathematical development of the RCR and mixed RCR models is referred to Appendix C. Extensions of currently available tests of hypotheses for determining model specification are included in Chapters 3 and 4 and may also be of interest to the technical reader. The results of Chapters 3 and 4 are then summarized in Chapter 5 so the non-technical reader can omit the mathematical development of the tests.

Section 2.2 Use of Residual Analysis to Determine Announcement Effects on Pricing of Common Stock

During recent years there has been an increase in the number of firms which have repurchased shares of their own common stock. One of the main concerns of those studying the increase in repurchasing activity is the pricing effect the repurchase will have on outstanding shares. The literature in this area indicates that, theoretically, repurchasing stock can have positive, neutral or negative price effects. The overall result depends, at least in part, on what the particular motivations to repurchase are (see Nantell and Finnerty, 1978).[1]

In a recent University of Michigan working paper Nantell and Finnerty (1974) examine the pricing effect from the repurchase of a firm's own shares.[2] They approach the problem using the methodology of "residual analysis." This methodology uses Sharpe's (1963) market model and an approach developed by Fama, Fisher, Jensen and Roll (1969) for isolating the effects of economic events on stock prices. The market model is a simple linear model specifying the return generating process for a specific security as follows:

$$R_{it} = a_i + b_i R_{mt} + e_{it} \qquad\qquad (2.1)$$

R_{it} = return to security i in time period t;

R_{mt} = market-wide return;

e_{it} = random disturbance or residual for security i in time period t;

a_i = an unknown constant term for firm i;

b_i = an unknown parameter viewed as an index of systematic risk for security i commonly called the "beta" coefficient.

The following procedure is typical of the residual analysis method of determining effects on pricing:

1) Estimate a_i and b_i for each security by ordinary least squares.
2) Compute the residuals around the date of repurchase announcement.
3) Compute the average residuals in each of the months around the announcement and plot these average residuals as a function of time period.

These plots are then examined for any "unusual" behavior of the residuals. This unusual behavior is defined as a significant difference from zero on the part of any of the average residuals. If, for example, the announcement has a positive effect on pricing, then the average residuals for the month of announcement should be significantly different from zero and this difference should be in a positive direction (see Appendix A for a more complete illustration and critique of residual analysis).

Residual analysis has proved to be a useful methodology for investigating many different announcement effects on pricing. As well as the repurchase announcement effect, it has been used to examine the effects of dividend announcement, stock splits (Fama, et al., 1969) and earnings announcements (Ball and Brown, 1968).

There are, however, other questions of interest in such studies that are often overlooked by researchers using residual analysis. Looking at the average residuals gives an indication of whether there is an overall effect for a number of firms in each time period. We might also want to say something about the size of the effect or examine in some manner how the effects are distributed across all firms. We might ask, for example, if there is a mean effect on pricing, whether this effect is positive, negative or zero, or how widely effects differ for the firms examined. Another question we might raise is whether firms exhibiting certain similar characteristics experience similar pricing effects. Does similarity in terms of size or debt ratio have some significance in determining such effects?

Management might be concerned with the effect on the risk of the stock as perceived by the market, i.e., the stock's beta coefficient. Does the announcement of a stock repurchase, or some other announcement which carries some information about the firm with it, result in an increase or decrease in the stock's beta? And is this change in the beta, if it occurs, maintained in the months following the announcement or does the beta value return to its previous level?

Many of these questions can be approached through the use of residual analysis but this task is often not a straightforward or an easy one. We therefore propose to examine alternative methodologies in order to study such pertinent financial questions.

Section 2.3 An Extension of the Residual Analysis Approach

As indicated in equation (2.1) of the previous section, the simple market model used in residual analysis can be written as:

$$R_{it} = a_i + b_i R_{mt} + e_{it} \qquad (2.2)$$

Announcement effects for such activities as a stock repurchase are measured by the residuals from the least squares fit for such a linear model. The determination of the significance of effects is generally approached in the following way: Find the arithmetic mean of the residuals for time period t for all N firms and see if this average effect differs significantly from zero. (See Appendix A).

Suppose we now consider an alternative approach to this method. We introduce a dummy variable into equation (2.2) by writing

$$R_{it} = a_i + b_i R_{mt} + c_{0,i} Z_{0;it} + e_{it} \qquad (2.3)$$

where

$$Z_{0;it} = \begin{cases} 1 \text{ if firm i made an announcement in period t} \\ 0 \text{ otherwise} \end{cases}$$

Now examine the least squares estimates of the parameters a_i, b_i and $c_{0,i}$.

The estimate of b_i, $\hat{b}_i$, will yield an indication of the systematic risk of stock i as before. The estimate of the constant term in the relationship is $\hat{a}_i$. Our new parameter, estimated as $\hat{c}_{0,i}$, will capture any unusual change in rate of return in the period of the repurchase announcement. The sign of $\hat{c}_{0,i}$ indicates whether the return for a stock has increased or decreased in the period of announcement.

Note that we can rewrite equation (2.3) as

$$R_{it} = a_i + b_i R_{mt} + e_{it}$$

when t is other than the period of repurchase announcement, and as

$$R_{it} = (a_i + c_{0,i}) + b_i R_{mt} + e_{it}$$

when t is equal to the period of announcement. We can represent these relationships graphically by two lines with differing intercepts as in Figure 2.1.

With most readily available regression programs the output will yield not only the parameter estimate, but will provide us with an estimate of both the standard error $s(\hat{c}_{0,i})$ and the value of the t-statistic for testing whether the population coefficient is different from zero.

What, if any, would be the advantages of such an approach over residual analysis? One of the main advantages stems from the versatility and ease of computation provided by the linear model. The method proposed here requires no computation of residuals; only the introduction of a dummy variable into our linear model. This task is usually very simply done with statistical packages providing regression routines. An additional advantage is that the use of this approach allows us to account for residual variances that may differ from one firm to another. Residual analysis ignores this fact. (See Appendix A for a more complete discussion and a test for overall repurchase effect.)

The versatility of the linear model approach will be demonstrated through several examples.

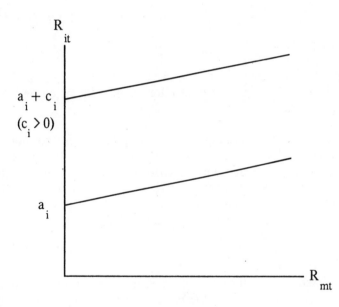

FIGURE 2.1
GRAPHICAL REPRESENTATION OF REPURCHASE EFFECT

Example 1

We may be interested not only in the pricing effect during the period of announcement but in other time periods around the announcement period. To determine pricing effects in the month preceding and the month following the announcement, we introduce two dummy variables $Z_{-1;it}$ and $Z_{+1;it}$ where

$$Z_{-1;it} = \begin{cases} 1 \text{ in the time period preceding any} \\ \quad \text{announcement made by firm i} \\ 0 \text{ otherwise} \end{cases}$$

and

$$Z_{+1;it} = \begin{cases} 1 \text{ in the time period following any} \\ \quad \text{announcement made by firm i} \\ 0 \text{ otherwise} \end{cases}$$

Our model becomes

$$R_{it} = a_i + b_i R_{mt} + c_{-1,i} Z_{-1;it} + c_{0,i} Z_{0;it} + c_{+1,i} Z_{+1;it} + e_{it} \qquad (2.4)$$

We can determine

1) anticipation effects by testing to see if $c_{-1,i}$ is equal to zero,
2) remainder effects in the period after announcement by testing to see if $c_{+1,i}$ is equal to zero.

Note the further advantage of this approach in relation to simultaneous tests of hypotheses. For example, using the F-test for full and reduced models (see Neter and Wasserman, 1974, pp. 259-65) we can test the simultaneous hypothesis H_o: $c_{-1,i} = c_{0,i} = c_{+1,i} = 0$. The procedure for such a test is very simple as can be noted in the previous reference.

Example 2

Suppose our interest is in the effect of a repurchase announcement on the beta coefficients of the stocks, the b_i. In particular, suppose we want to determine whether there is a shift in the beta coefficient at the time of the repurchase announcement. To the simple market model we add the new variable

$$S_{i,t} = \begin{cases} 0 \text{ in the time periods before any} \\ \quad \text{announcement is made by firm i} \\ R_{mt} \text{ in the period of announcement} \\ \quad \text{and in those time periods following .} \end{cases}$$

Our model is

$$R_{it} = a_i + b_i R_{mt} + c_i S_{i,t} + e_{it} \qquad (2.5)$$

Note here that the beta coefficient for stock i has been decomposed into two parts:

$$\text{beta} = \begin{cases} b_i & \text{in the time periods before any} \\ & \text{announcement by firm i} \\ b_i + c_i & \text{in the time period of announcement} \\ & \text{and in those time periods following .} \end{cases}$$

Beta is the sum of the effects accounted for by R_{mt} with the overall effect being split into two parts beginning with the announcement date.

To determine whether a change has occurred in the beta coefficient we can use $\hat{c}_i$, our estimated value of c_i, to test the hypothesis: H_0: $c_i = 0$.

Example 3

If we believe that the change in the beta coefficient occurs as a trend after announcement rather than as a sudden shift, we can test for such an effect as follows:

Define a new variable $D_{i,t}$ as

$$D_{i,t} = \begin{cases} 0 & \text{in the time periods before any} \\ & \text{announcement is made by firm i} \\ (t - t_0) \cdot R_{mt} & \text{in the period of announcement} \\ & \text{and in those time periods following,} \\ & \text{i.e., multiply the value for the market} \\ & \text{return in each time period from the} \\ & \text{announcement on by the number, t,} \\ & \text{of that period minus the number, } t_0, \\ & \text{of the announcement period.} \end{cases}$$

Our model becomes

$$R_{it} = a_i + b_i R_{mt} + c_i D_{i,t} + e_{it} \qquad (2.6)$$

The significance of the least squares estimate of c_i will tell us if a trend in the beta values exists and the sign of the coefficient will tell us if the trend is positive or negative.

The use of such a trend variable in the regression equations can be more clearly pictured by again thinking of the beta coefficient in equation (2.6) as having been decomposed into two parts:

$$
\text{beta} = \begin{cases} b_i & \text{in the time periods before any} \\ & \text{announcement by firm i} \\ b_i + c_i \ (t - t_0) & \text{in the time period of announcement} \\ & \text{and in those time periods following.} \end{cases}
$$

Beta is the sum of the effects accounted for by R_{mt} with the overall effect being split into two parts, as in the previous example, beginning with the announcement date.

The versatility of such an approach should be clear from the preceding examples. The method is convenient because test statistics are calculated by most regression programs and thus avoids some computational effort in working with residuals.

Despite the versatility and computational ease of the linear model approach suggested in this section there are still drawbacks that can be pointed out. We are still dealing with the firms one by one. Tests of significance are performed on the individual coefficients. A further disadvantage is due to the large number of parameters to be estimated. Referring again to equation (2.1) we see that there are two regression parameters to be estimated for each stock; the slope of the regression line or the beta coefficient, b_i, and the intercept a_i. Also, in order to construct tests of hypotheses about coefficients we need an estimate of the variance around the regression line. We denote this variance for stock i by σ_i^2 and its estimate by $\hat{\sigma}_i^2$. Note that this allows the variation for each of the N securities to differ. Thus in any one of the regressions performed to estimate the parameters a_i, b_i and σ_i^2 we must estimate a total of three parameters with T observations. As we add dummy variables to the above equation we increase the number of parameters while the number of observations remains fixed. If it were somehow possible to reduce the number of parameter estimates needed while maintaining a fixed number of observations, we could achieve greater efficiency in our regression estimates.

In the following section we introduce the idea of constructing a model which deals with all N firms by pooling the N cross-sections of time series observations. Several different models suggested in the recent econometric literature are examined and reviewed along with the advantages and disadvantages of each.

**Section 2.4   Pooling Cross-Sectional and Time Series Data
in a Financial Analysis**

Availability of data on a large number of individuals (firms, households,
etc.) over a number of periods of time is becoming increasingly common
in business and economics. A case in point is the stock market data to
which we have been referring. Here the individuals are the N firms.
We have observed the rates of return, R_{it}, for the stock of each firm over
T time periods. As such data becomes more common, better methods
of analysis are being sought. If we analyze each firm separately we are
using T observations to estimate the parameters in each firm model.
After running N regressions of this type we are left with the problem of
analyzing the resulting parameter estimates in a coherent fashion. Such
an analysis is difficult especially when N is large. Rather than using such
a firm-by-firm analysis, the econometric literature is suggesting some type
of pooled approach. By pooling the data at hand we will be working at
one time with all N times series of T observations each, thus increasing
the base of our data considerably. These N·T observations used in a
single more general model should provide relatively more efficient
parameter estimates as well as a more meaningful interpretation of what
is happening across all N firms for the time periods in question. We
would also hope to have the ability to make inferences to the population
from which our sample of N firms was drawn.

Several approaches to dealing with pooled cross-sectional and time
series data have been presented in the recent literature. A review of those
methods of major importance will be presented in the following text.

1. The Extremes

There are three methods which have been used in the past which we will
classify as "extremes" in working with data available for individual units
over a number of periods of time. The first has been demonstrated in
the preceding discussion.

1A. Separate Firm Regressions. We assume a specific linear model
with K parameters of interest for each firm, then estimate the K
parameters separately for each firm.

Writing the models as

$$R_{it} = \sum_{k=0}^{K-1} b_{ik} X_{itk} + e_{it}$$

(2.7)

where $i = 1, \ldots, N; \ t = 1, \ldots, T$

we see that this approach involves performing N time series regressions and results in the estimation of N·K parameters. We are implicitly assuming by the use of this method that the parameters, b_{ik}, for each of the N firms are fixed but different. (Note that this method cannot be classed as a "true" pooled analysis since we are operating with each cross-section individually.) The problems existing with the use of this extreme method have already been mentioned.

A modification of the use of separate firm regressions is Zellner's (1962) Seemingly Unrelated Regressions (SUR) approach. Given a set of regression equations, Zellner notes that only under certain special conditions will OLS, performed equation by equation, yield parameter estimates that are relatively efficient (efficient in the sense of having a smaller standard error than any other estimation procedure).[3] Although Zellner's approach is applicable to other than pooled cross-sectional and time series data it seems especially useful in this case.

If we have a set of N time series regression equations written as:

$$R_{1t} = \sum_{k=0}^{K-1} b_{1k} x_{1tk} + e_{1t}$$

(2.8)

$$R_{Nt} = \sum_{k=0}^{K-1} b_{Nk} X_{Ntk} + e_{Nt}$$

there are only two cases when OLS applied to each equation individually will yield efficient estimates.

For this to happen it must be true that either: (1) the regressors of each equation must lie in the same space, in particular, when each individual equation involves exactly the same explanatory variables; or (2) no correlation exists between disturbance terms in different equations.

The first condition can be seen to hold in our set of equations involving the simple market model:

$$R_{it} = a_i + b_i R_{mt} + e_{it}$$

(2.9)

Here the same explanatory variables (a term for the constant effect and R_{mt}) appear in each equation. However, when a model such as that in equation (2.3) in the previous section is considered, our situation changes.   Unless there is only one repurchase announcement for each firm and this announcement occurs in exactly the same time period for all N firms, the introduction of the $Z_{o;it}$ dummy variable will violate condition (1) above.   In such instances as this where condition (1) does not hold, there may be a subtle connection between the N separate equations.   This connection is in the contemporaneous correlation (a correlation between cross-sections) of the disturbance terms.   The subtlety of this link is the reason behind the name; the regressions are "seemingly" unrelated.

Zellner (1962) provides us with a generalized least squares (GLS) approach to the estimation of such a set of regression equations which utilizes any correlation existing between the separate cross-section error terms.   The use of this added information provides estimates of the parameters that are asymptotically more efficient than would be obtained using equation by equation ordinary least squares estimation.   Zellner proves this fact in his paper.   There have been a number of studies examining the small sample properties of Zellner's SUR approach. These are reviewed briefly in Appendix B.

1B.   Classical Pooling. Zellner's SUR approach does provide us with a relatively more efficient estimation technique than equation by equation OLS.   It does not, however, remedy all the problems mentioned for the first extreme method.   We are still faced with analyzing in a coherent fashion the N·K parameter estimates which result.

Opposed to the first extreme of estimating N·K fixed but different parameters is the second of our extreme methods.   If we assume the parameters in question to be equal for all N firms we can approach the problem of estimation by pooling all of our data and performing a single ordinary least squares regression.   We are in this case estimating only K parameters and will have increased the number of observations used to do this as well as the number of degrees of freedom in any statistical tests performed.   We write this model as

$$R_{it} = \sum_{k=0}^{K-1} b_k X_{itk} + e_{it}$$

(2.10)

where $i = 1, \ldots, N;\ t = 1, \ldots, T.$

It should be noted here that, in principle, we could use T separate cross-section regressions or N separate time-series regressions to obtain estimates of the b_k.   If the b_k are constant over both time and cross-sectional units, however, we would rather pool all the observations and run a single regression for the sake of statistical efficiency (Pindyck and Rubinfeld, 1976, p. 203).

The drawback of this second extreme method of analysis is simply that the b_k may differ between cross-sectional units, in which case our model is improperly specified and the coefficient estimates will be biased. We must also assume that the e_{it} are independently distributed with mean zero and variance σ^2. Otherwise the use of generalized least squares estimation may be needed.

1C. Aggregation of Individual Relationships. Aggregation of relationships pertaining to individuals (microrelations), say, firms, in order to obtain a relationship for the group as a whole (a macrorelation) is a third method of analyzing pooled cross-sectional and time series data which will be classified as an extreme. Using the market model, the concept of aggregation will be illustrated and the problems associated with the technique will be discussed.

Our microrelation is given by the market model itself. For firm i we have

$$R_{it} = a_i + b_i R_{mt} + e_{it}. \qquad (2.11)$$

We introduce macrovariables

$$\overline{R}_t = \frac{1}{N}\sum_{i=1}^{N} R_{it} \, , \; \overline{R}_{mt} = \frac{1}{N}\sum_{i=1}^{N} R_{mt} = R_{mt} \, , \qquad (2.12)$$

i.e., we average the variables pertaining to the individual firms over all N firms for each time period t.

If $a_1 = a_2 = \ldots = a_n = \overline{a}$ and $b_1 = b_2 = \ldots = b_n = \overline{b}$ we can construct the macrorelation

$$\overline{R}_t = \overline{a} + \overline{b} R_{mt} + \frac{1}{N}\sum_{i=1}^{N} e_{it} \qquad (2.13)$$

and use OLS to estimate the coefficients of this group relationship. If the microcoefficients are not all equal, OLS estimation of $\overline{a}$ and $\overline{b}$ will result in what is termed an aggregation bias. This would be the case in working with our individual firm relationships since we know the systematic risk of the individual stocks (b_i) will differ from one firm to another. For a complete discussion of aggregation and aggregation bias see Theil (1971, pp. 556-62).

2. The Covariance or Dummy Variable Model

In an attempt to relax the stringent assumption that individual firm coefficients remain constant (1B and 1C), and yet improving on the technique of separate regressions (1A), several models have been proposed. The models discussed in this section and the next allow the equation intercepts to vary as a means of representing individual firm (and/or time) effects. The first of these models, the covariance or dummy variable model, attempts to improve the specification of the model we termed a classical pooled regression by the introduction of dummy variables (see Wallace and Hussain, 1969, Pindyck and Rubinfeld, 1976, pp. 203-6). The use of the dummy variables is an attempt to adjust for missing information in the model. In this approach we accept the equality of the slope coefficients from one firm to another but we assume the intercepts differ from firm to firm. So we introduce dummy variables such as

$$W_{it} = \begin{cases} 1 \text{ for firm } i \\ 0 \text{ otherwise} \end{cases}$$

for $i = 2, \ldots, N$

into the classical pooled model (2.10) to obtain

$$R_{it} = a + \sum_{k=1}^{K} b_k X_{itk} + \sum_{i=2}^{N} c_i W_{it} + e_{it} \cdot {}^{4} \tag{2.14}$$

where the constraint $\sum_{i=2}^{N} c_i = 0$ is imposed.

We thus allow the intercept to vary with respect to cross-sectional unit.

The estimation of such a model using ordinary least squares would have the following results:

a) Estimates of all parameters would be unbiased provided that the usual assumptions are satisfied.
b) The OLS estimates of c_i would provide measurements of the change in the cross-section intercepts.

3. The Error Components Model

The problems existing with the covariance model are clearly evident: First of all the slope coefficients, b_k, are still assumed constant for all firms. Secondly, there are a substantial number of parameters to be estimated thus using up a large number of degrees of freedom. And, finally, the coefficients of the dummy variables are not easily interpretable. They represent, as Maddala (1971) points out, "some ignorance — just like the residuals e_{it}." We do not specify variables which might cause the regression line to shift; we are simply inserting dummy variables to measure such shifts. Maddala then suggests that this "specific ignorance" might just as well be treated in a manner similar to that of our "general ignorance" (e_{it}). In other words, we could view the term c_i as a normally distributed random variable with mean zero and unknown variance. As well as achieving consistency in the incorporation of our "ignorance" into the model, this approach would also decrease the number of parameters to be estimated. Such a model has become known as the variance components or error components model. This model can be written as

$$R_{it} = (a + c_i) + \sum_{k=1}^{K-1} b_k X_{itk} + e_{it} \qquad (2.15)$$

where

   a is the overall mean (or fixed component of the intercept), c_i is the random component of the intercept over individual units, and the remaining model components are the same as previously specified.

   We can rewrite (1.15) as

$$R_{it} = a + \sum_{k=1}^{K-1} b_k X_{itk} + w_{it} \qquad (2.16)$$

where

$$w_{it} = c_i + e_{it} \qquad (2.17)$$

thus combining the random components into a single disturbance term.[5] The error components model then becomes a special case of the general linear model with non-scalar residual covariance matrix, i.e., the covariance matrix of w_{it} can no longer be written as a constant, σ^2, times the identity matrix. The non-zero correlation that exists between w_{it} and w_{is} (between the residuals of a given cross-sectional unit at two different points in time) results in non-zero off-diagonal elements in the covariance matrix. Ordinary least squares will no longer provide efficient parameter estimates as it would under the assumptions of the classical pooled model (1B) or the covariance model (2). A form of generalized least squares regression is needed to improve the relative efficiency of the estimates. The construction of GLS estimators typically proceeds by using a two-step procedure. The OLS residuals are obtained at the first step and are used to estimate the covariance structure. The second step consists of transforming the variables in the model in such a way that the correlation structure is altered to meet OLS assumptions; then using OLS on the transformed variables to obtain the GLS estimates of the parameters (see Johnston, 1972, pp. 208-13 for the GLS transformation in general; and Nerlove, 1971a, for the procedure specific to the error components model).

A considerable amount of analytic work has been published dealing with the error components model. Wallace and Hussain (1969), Nerlove (1971a), Maddala (1971), Arora (1973), Amemiya (1971), Balestra and Nerlove (1966), and Swamy and Arora (1972), have examined this model analytically. Nerlove (1971a), Maddala and Mount (1973), and Arora (1973), have done Monte Carlo studies examining the small sample properties of different estimation techniques. When the independent variables are non-stochastic there are a variety of techniques for constructing the GLS coefficient estimator which seem to work equally well. With a lagged value of the dependent variable as an explanatory variable, Nerlove (1971a) has a clearly superior method of constructing the estimator. The research concerning small sample properties has been reviewed in more detail in a working paper by Dielman and Wright (1977).

4. The Random Coefficient Regression Model

The error components model provides an alternative to the firm by firm analysis used in the residual analysis methodology. It is an improvement over the covariance model due to the reduction in the number of parameters to be estimated. Unfortunately, however, the use of the error components model has not alleviated one especially restrictive assumption: We assume that the slope coefficients, b_{ik}, for each firm are equal. This may be an acceptable assumption in certain applications, but is often violated in working with the models of our financial data. For example, in the model

$$R_{it} = a_i + b_i R_{mt} + e_{it} \qquad (2.18)$$

this assumption would require that the beta coefficients, b_i, be equal for all stocks. This would clearly be too great a simplification in most analyses.

We are thus led to search for an approach allowing the coefficients of interest to differ between firms. Still, we hope to provide some method of modeling the firms as a group rather than individually.

One possibility would be to introduce dummy variables into our model that would indicate differences in the coefficients across individual units, i.e., develop an approach similar to the covariance model (see Maddala, 1977, p. 324). Such a dummy variable approach would prove unwieldly if there were many coefficients or many individual units, however, due to the large number of parameters to be estimated. It is generally better to generalize the error components model still further, treating not just the intercept but all the coefficients as random in those cases where such a model seems appropriate. Maddala's (1971) intuitive argument for the error components pooling procedure (summarized above) can be extended to those procedures that also treat the slope coefficients as random. When using the dummy variable or covariance approach we are ignoring any between group variance and simply measuring the differences in the coefficients for different time or individual units. In the classical pooling approach (1B), on the other hand, the between group and within group variation is just added up. We are thus resorting to "all or nothing ways" of utilizing this variation. An approach assuming the coefficients to be random is a compromise solution to that of treating them as being all the same (classical pooling) or all different (covariance). This section will examine a random coefficient regression model appropriate to the analysis of our financial data.

Again we consider the simplest case of the market model:

$$R_{it} = a_i + b_i R_{mt} + e_{it} \qquad (2.19)$$

where $i = 1, \ldots, N; t = 1, \ldots, T$.

Suppose we now allow each regression coefficient to vary between stocks, viewing both a_i and b_i as random variables. We view both coefficients as invariant over time, but varying from stock to stock. We can also assume particular distributions for these random variables for purposes of inference but this is not necessary for out present discussion. The coefficients a_i and b_i can be rewritten as

$$a_i = \bar{a} + c_i$$
$$b_i = \bar{b} + v_i \qquad\qquad (2.20)$$

where $\bar{a}$ and $\bar{b}$ are fixed components, the means of the distributions from which each coefficient is drawn, and v_i and c_i are random components with mean zero. The components c_i and v_i allow the coefficients to differ from firm to firm.

Using the above notation we can write the RCR model as

$$R_{it} = (\bar{a} + c_i) + (\bar{b} + v_i) R_{mt} + e_{it}$$

$$= \bar{a} + \bar{b} R_{mt} + w_{it} \qquad\qquad (2.21)$$

$$\text{where } w_{it} = c_i + v_i R_{mt} + e_{it}. \qquad\qquad (2.22)$$

As in the error components model we can combine the random components into a single disturbance term. We are again faced with a nonspherical disturbance covariance matrix and find that a generalized least squares estimator will provide more efficient estimates of $\bar{a}$ and $\bar{b}$ than a technique such as classical pooling.

The model in equations (2.19) or (2.21) (in a more general form) is the Random Coefficient Regression (RCR) model examined by Swamy in several recent publications. The statistical estimation procedure he developed is again a two-step procedure (see Feige and Swamy, 1974; Swamy, 1970, 1971, 1973, 1974). First, separate regression equations are calculated for each stock. Then the population mean and variance for the distributions of each regression coefficient are estimated. The estimates of the population means are a complicated weighted average of the OLS estimates of each individual coefficient. The weights used involve both the standard error of each regression and the covariance structure of the random coefficients. The variances of the coefficients are estimated as a sample variance of the individually estimated coefficients allowing for variation arising from the residuals, e_{it}, in the model. Maddala (1977, p. 330) points out that the random coefficient approach is different from the variance components approach in the following way. In the variance components model we treat the intercepts as random because we consider them to be a combination of factors about which we are ignorant. They are then treated as we treat the residuals. In the random coefficient regression model we assume the slope coefficients are random and drawn from a distribution with a certain mean and variance. Our interest lies in making inferences about this mean and variance. We are concerned with the population of coefficients and in gathering information to describe this population specifically. The information gathered about the intercepts in the variance components model is merely used to adjust the estimates of the slope coefficients.

In the following examples we illustrate the power of Swamy's approach in a financial analysis examining our stock repurchase data. We refer to two examples discussed earlier.

Example 1

First we consider the effects of announcement of a stock repurchase using a sample of N firms. To determine the effects of this event on the rates of return we will again resort to the introduction of dummy variables into the simple market model. Define the dummy variable $Z_{0;it}$ as

$$Z_{0;it} = \begin{cases} 1 \text{ if firm i made an announcement in period t} \\ 0 \text{ otherwise} \end{cases}$$

Our model then becomes

$$R_{it} = a_i + b_i R_{mt} + c_{o,i} Z_{0;it} + e_{it} \tag{2.23}$$

Viewing the coefficients in equation (2.23) as random and applying Swamy's estimation techniques will yield estimates of the means ($\bar{a}$, $\bar{b}$ and $\bar{c}_o$) as well as estimates of the variances of the coefficients ($V(a_i)$, $V(b_i)$ and $V(c_{o,i})$).

The coefficient $c_{o,i}$ in this model indicates any shift in the rate of return for stock i in the period of repurchase announcement. The mean of these shift coefficients, $\bar{c}_o$, tells us the average effect of repurchase announcement while $V(c_{o,i})$ yields an indication of the variation from stock to stock of these changes.

Recall that in the dummy variable approach specified in the previous section we required estimates of a_i, b_i and $c_{o,i}$ for each of the N firms. In our random coefficient pooled analysis we are interested only in estimates of the means and variances (or standard deviations) of the population distributions of the coefficients. We are thus reducing the number of parameters to be estimated from N to 2 for each coefficient. The pooled analysis also allows us $N \cdot T$ observations with which to work, thus expanding the base of our data.

Also note that inference to population parameters (in particular, population means) is possible using the RCR model. In the firm-by-firm analysis, we obtained coefficient estimates of the effects of repurchase announcement for each stock and were left with the task of determining when a sufficient number of these effects were significant for an overall market effect to have occurred or, alternatively, of forming some value felt to be an appropriate indication of the mean effect and determining the significance of this value. By using the RCR approach we no longer have to deal with such problems. To determine the significance of an overall or market effect we concern ourselves with the estimate of the mean effect, $\hat{\bar{c}}_o$. Our estimate is an unbiased estimate of the population mean effect $\bar{c}_o$. The problem of analyzing an overall effect can thus be undertaken by testing hypotheses about $\bar{c}_o$.

Example 2

We now confront the problem of determining what effect the repurchase announcement has on the stocks' beta coefficients, the b_i. We might be faced with the question of whether this index of risk increases, decreases or shows no change as a result of the announcement. Again we are concerned with an overall effect rather than the effect on individual stocks. We introduce the variable

$$
S_t \;=\; \begin{cases} 0 \text{ in the time periods before any} \\ \quad \text{announcement made by firm i} \\ R_{mt} \;\; \text{in the period of announcement} \\ \quad \text{and in those time periods following.} \end{cases}
$$

Our model becomes

$$R_{it} = a_i + b_i R_{mt} + c_i S_t + e_{it} \tag{2.24}$$

The estimates of c_i indicate, for each firm, the shift in the beta coefficient at the time of announcement if one does occur. Using the RCR approach we estimate the mean effect by $\hat{\bar{c}}$ and the variation from stock to stock by $\hat{V}(c_i)$. The significance of this mean effect tells us whether we can conclude that any change occurs in the average systematic risk of stocks as a result of a repurchase announcement.

An advantage of the RCR approach involves simultaneous inference about several of the parameters in the model. Using the techniques to be developed in Chapter 3 we will have the ability to simultaneously test hypotheses about any subset of the parameters.

Although the examples presented in this chapter deal exclusively with the introduction of dummy variables into the market model, we are not restricted to this approach. Structural variables such as change in captial structure or size of the repurchase can be introduced. Hypotheses can then be framed to test whether these structural variables help to explain repurchase announcement effects or firm-to-firm variation in the beta coefficients (see Rosenberg, 1974, and Rosenberg and McKibben, 1973). This capability is another advantage of the linear model approach.

5. The Mixed RCR Model

Application of the RCR techniques to the modeling of financial data provides estimates of the coefficient means and variances. The variance estimates obtained from this type of analysis are sometimes very small for certain coefficients and the estimation procedures used can yield negative estimates of variance (see Wright et al., 1977a, 1977b). Swamy (1971, pp. 147-49) suggests two possibilities in these cases:

(1) the model may be misspecified.
(2) we may have coefficients in the model that are not random.

Negative variance estimates can result from the estimators used in certain instances when the form of the variance-covariance matrix of the disturbance terms in the model is not correctly specified. (Misspecification may occur in assumptions made about homoscedasticity, serial correlation or contemporaneous correlation.) When the assumptions made are believed to be reasonable and the variance estimates remain small or negative, we may want to consider certain coefficients in the model to be fixed. There are also statistical procedures available to test for such a possibility. We shall call a model containing both fixed and random coefficients a mixed random coefficient regression model (mixed RCR model).[6]

The mixed RCR model is our next step in models useful for analyzing pooled data. Suppose, for example, we are evaluating market effects of a repurchase announcement using the model

$$R_{it} = a_i + b_i R_{mt} + c_{o,i} Z_{0;it} + e_{it} \qquad (2.25)$$

We first estimate the model assuming all coefficients are random but we find that the estimated variance of a_i, $\hat{V}(a_i)$, is near zero. Perhaps we also have some statistical procedure to test the hypothesis H_0: $V(a_i) = 0$ and the resulting test statistic tells us to accept H_0.

We would then want to re-estimte the coefficients under the mixed RCR assumptions. Our model would be

$$R_{it} = a + b_i\, R_{mt} + c_{o,i}\, Z_{0:it} + e_{it} \qquad\qquad (2.26)$$

The coefficient a does not vary from stock to stock as with the RCR approach.

This extension of the RCR model is important for both estimation and inference. This point is stressed in the final section of Chapter 3. As will be noted there, estimating the mean of a coefficient assumed random, say $\bar{a}$ and estimating the coefficient as a fixed parameter, a, can yield widely differing values. (One of these choices must be a misspecification since the parameter cannot be both random and fixed.) Inferences about $\bar{a}$ and a may also differ. Analytic results in Chapter 3 will show that misspecifying a coefficient as random when it is actually fixed can lead to inferential conclusions about that particular coefficient that are clearly wrong. Thus, it is important to allow for the possibility of both fixed and random parameters in the model. We have previously seen one example of a mixed RCR model in the error components (3) model. In this case the intercept was assumed to vary from stock to stock and the slope coefficients were all assumed to be fixed across stocks.

The mixed RCR model will be examined analytically in subsequent chapters and estimation techniques developed by Swamy (1971, pp. 143-55) will be referred to on several occasions. To save the interested reader from searching out this reference we have chosen to include the necessary results in Appendix C.

Section 2.5 Summary

Residual analysis has been the standard technique of empirical researchers in the field of finance for examining the effect of economic events on stock prices and rates of return. Due to drawbacks in the technique we proposed the use of an alternative approach to examine such effects. First, we extended the market model so that coefficients rather than residuals could be used to indicate changes in rate of return. This provided formulas for the direct calculation of standard errors and significance of individual effects. Next, we reviewed the econometrics literature in an attempt to find models which would allow us to combine the results from individual firms in order to obtain an indication of the overall or market effect of the event on rate of return. The models suggested as appropriate for analyzing pooled cross-sectional and time series data were:

1) The extremes:
   A) Separate Equation Regressions
      Seemingly Unrelated Regressions
   B) Classical Pooling
   C) Aggregation
2) Covariance Analysis
3) Error Components
4) Random Coefficient Regression
5) Mixed Random Coefficient Regression

The RCR and mixed RCR models seemed worthy of strong recommendation in proposed analyses of stock market data. They are versatile in the types of problems with which they can deal. They also provide a coherent method for making inferences about certain population parameters of interest from a sample of firms. As will be seen in Chapter 6, the mixed RCR model is both a feasible alternative to the residual analysis approach and can provide insights which would not be possible using residual analysis alone.

Chapter 3

Mixed Random Coefficient Regression Models: Extension of Methodology

In Chapter 2 we progressed through a number of different models useful in analyzing market data. The majority of these dealt with some manner of pooling the data rather than analyzing relationships for each individual firm. This idea is attractive when we are concerned with overall market effects rather than the effects felt by each firm viewed as a separate entity. Justification was made for the use of a random coefficient model in such cases. When regression coefficients vary from firm to firm, the RCR model allows us to view them as randomly distributed across firms. We can then describe the distribution of each coefficient by estimating a few population parameters. In this way we will have described the overall or market behavior of coefficients and, thus, the effects measured by these coefficients. If, however, the relationship between any dependent and explanatory variable is fixed across all firms, then the RCR model is no longer appropriate. Our remedy for such a situation was to allow both fixed and random coefficients in our regression models leading to our discussion of the mixed RCR model. The usefulness of the mixed RCR model in any analysis will, of course, depend on the availability and quality of techniques capable of helping us to determine the most appropriate model specification. The inference techniques associated with the mixed model have not been very extensively documented. Also, tests of several important hypotheses have been neglected in the literature. In this light we propose a twofold purpose for this chapter:

1) To develop tests of some hypotheses pertaining to model specification, and
2) To compare the behavior of t-statistics for
   a) testing whether the mean of a random coefficient is different from zero and
   b) testing whether a fixed coefficient is different from zero.

For the purposes of the work to be done in this chapter we abandon the notational convention of the previous chapter. Results will not be presented in terms of the rates of return, R_{it}, and the explanatory variables used in our stock repurchase example. Rather, we move to the more general formulation commonly seen throughout statistics books and journals and adopt vector and matrix notation.

Section 3.1   Extension of Hypothesis Testing Techniques

Referring to the mathematical presentation of the mixed RCR model in Appendix C we extend the Swamy model given in (C.1),

$$\underline{Y}_i = X_{1i}\,\underline{b}_{1i} + X_{2i}\,\underline{b}_2 + \underline{e}_i \qquad (3.1)$$

$$i = 1, \ \ldots, \ N \ ,$$

by partitioning the vector of random coefficients and rewriting the model as

$$\underline{Y}_i = Z_{1i}\,\underline{\gamma}_{1i} + Z_{2i}\,\underline{\gamma}_{2i} + X_{2i}\,\underline{b}_2 + \underline{e}_i \qquad (3.2)$$

$$\text{where} \quad \underline{b}_{1i} \;=\; \begin{bmatrix} \underline{\gamma}_{1i} \\[2mm] \underline{\gamma}_{2i} \end{bmatrix} \quad ; \qquad\qquad (3.3)$$

$$X_{1i} \;=\; \begin{bmatrix} Z_{1i} \\[2mm] Z_{2i} \end{bmatrix} \quad ; \qquad\qquad (3.4)$$

$\underline{\gamma}_{1i}$ is an $H_1 \times 1$ vector of random coefficients to be included in a test of some hypothesis;

$\underline{\gamma}_{2i}$ is an $H_2 \times 1$ vector of random coefficients, but these are excluded from the test;

$\underline{b}_2$ is a $K_2 \times 1$ vector of fixed coefficients;

$\underline{Y}_i$ is a $T \times 1$ vector of observations on the dependent variable;

$\overline{Z}_{1i}$, Z_{2i} and X_{2i} are matrices of observations on the independent variables and are dimensioned as $T \times H_1$, $T \times H_2$ and $T \times K_2$, respectively; $\underline{e}_i$ is a $T \times 1$ vector of random disturbances.

We make the following assumptions concerning the model in (3.2):

(1) $T > H_1 + H_2 + K_2 = K_1 + K_2 = K$
(2) rank $(Z_{1i}) = H_1$, rank $(Z_{2i}) = H_2$, rank $(X_{2i}) = K_2$

$$(3)\ \underline{b}_{1i} = \begin{bmatrix} \underline{\gamma}_{1i} \\ \underline{\gamma}_{2i} \end{bmatrix} \sim iid\ N\left(\begin{bmatrix} \bar{\underline{\gamma}}_1 \\ \bar{\underline{\gamma}}_2 \end{bmatrix}, \begin{bmatrix} \Delta_1 & \Delta_{12} \\ \Delta_{21} & \Delta_2 \end{bmatrix} \right)$$

(4) $\underline{e}_i \sim N(\underline{0}, \sigma_{ii} I_T)$;
(5) $\underline{\gamma}_{1i}$ and $\underline{\gamma}_{2i}$ are independent of $\underline{e}_i$.

Following Swamy's convention of writing the random coefficients as a fixed component, $\bar{\underline{\gamma}}_j$, plus a random component, $\underline{\delta}_j$, (see Equation (C.2) in Appendix C) our model can now be rewritten by combining the N equations of (3.2) into a single model:

$$\underline{Y} = Z_1 \bar{\underline{\gamma}}_1 + Z_2 \bar{\underline{\gamma}}_2 + X_2 \underline{b}_2 + \underline{u} \tag{3.5}$$

where $\underline{u} = D(Z_1) \underline{\delta}_1 + D(Z_2) \underline{\delta}_2 + \underline{e}$. $\tag{3.6}$

Notation in the above form of our model is as follows:

$$\underline{Y} = \begin{bmatrix} \underline{Y}_1 \\ \underline{Y}_2 \\ \vdots \\ \underline{Y}_N \end{bmatrix},\ Z_1 = \begin{bmatrix} Z_{11} \\ Z_{12} \\ \vdots \\ Z_{1N} \end{bmatrix},\ Z_2 = \begin{bmatrix} Z_{21} \\ Z_{22} \\ \vdots \\ Z_{2N} \end{bmatrix},\ X_2 = \begin{bmatrix} X_{21} \\ X_{22} \\ \vdots \\ X_{2N} \end{bmatrix}, \tag{3.7}$$

$$D(Z_j) = \begin{bmatrix} Z_{j1} & 0 & - - - & 0 \\ 0 & Z_{j2} & - - - & 0 \\ \vdots & \vdots & \ddots & \vdots \\ 0 & 0 & - - - & Z_{jN} \end{bmatrix}\ j = 1,2 \tag{3.8}$$

$$\underline{\delta}_1 = \begin{bmatrix} \underline{\delta}_{11} \\ \underline{\delta}_{12} \\ \vdots \\ \underline{\delta}_{1N} \end{bmatrix}, \quad \underline{\delta}_2 = \begin{bmatrix} \underline{\delta}_{21} \\ \underline{\delta}_{22} \\ \vdots \\ \underline{\delta}_{2N} \end{bmatrix}, \quad \underline{e} = \begin{bmatrix} \underline{e}_1 \\ \vdots \\ \underline{e}_N \end{bmatrix}. \tag{3.9}$$

In this model we write the variance-covariance matrix of the disturbance term $\underline{u}$ as

$$\text{Var}(\underline{u}) = \Sigma. \tag{3.10}$$

In Appendix C we have summarized Swamy's presentation of this model. Estimation techniques developed in his book, *Statistical Inference in Random Coefficient Regression Models*, are reviewed and existing hypothesis tests are noted.

The deficiencies in these tests are clearly evident from consideration of the general model we presented in (3.5). Only tests of the full vector of coefficient means, $\bar{\underline{b}}_1$, are considered. We may, however, be concerned with tests of significance on only a subset of the coefficients considered random in the model, i.e., on a partition, $\bar{\underline{\gamma}}_1$, of the full mean vector. The same problem arises for tests of randomness. Perhaps we believe that H_2 of the coefficients are random but are unsure of some other H_1 of the coefficients in our model. Our test then involves only a partition of the full vector of random coefficients.

A further desirable extension would be a simultaneous test that a coefficient or set of coefficients is non-random *and* equal to zero. If such an hypothesis were accepted we would certainly want to drop the variables corresponding to these coefficients from our model. In cases where the coefficient is fixed and non-zero or random with mean zero, the corresponding variables would still be explaining some variation and, thus, adding to the explanatory power of the model.

We now put these suggested hypotheses into a more formal statement and develop appropriate tests in each case.

A. A test for partitions of the mean vector.

Given the model in (3.5),

$$\underline{Y} = Z_1 \underline{\bar{\gamma}}_1 + Z_2 \underline{\bar{\gamma}}_2 + X_2 \underline{b}_2 + \underline{u}, \tag{3.11}$$

the hypothesis we wish to test is

$$H_o: \underline{\bar{\gamma}}_1 = \underline{\bar{\gamma}}_{10}$$

$$\text{vs. } H_a: \underline{\bar{\gamma}}_1 \neq \underline{\bar{\gamma}}_{10} \tag{3.12}$$

where $\underline{\bar{\gamma}}_{10}$ is a vector of preassigned values.

The test statistic can be written as

$$F = \frac{(N - H_1)}{H_1 (N-1)} (\underline{\hat{\bar{\gamma}}}_1 - \underline{\bar{\gamma}}_{10})' \, V(\underline{\hat{\bar{\gamma}}}_1)^{-1} (\underline{\hat{\bar{\gamma}}}_1 - \underline{\bar{\gamma}}_{10}) \tag{3.13}$$

where $\underline{\hat{\bar{\gamma}}}_1$ is the mixed RCR estimate of $\underline{\bar{\gamma}}_1$ and $V(\underline{\hat{\bar{\gamma}}}_1)^{-1}$ is that inverse of the partition of the estimated variance-covariance matrix of the coefficients corresponding to the partition $\underline{\bar{\gamma}}_1$.
      Under H_o, F has, asymptotically, the F-distribution with H_1 and $N\text{-}H_1$ degrees of freedom.

Proof:

Referring to models (C.1) and (C.4) in Appendix C, we have

$$\underline{Y}_i = X_{1i} \underline{b}_{1i} + X_{2i} \underline{b}_2 + \underline{e}_i \tag{3.14}$$

$$\text{and } \underline{Y} = X_1 \underline{\bar{b}}_1 + X_2 \underline{b}_2 + \underline{u}. \tag{3.15}$$

Swamy (1971, p. 117-18) has shown that

$$(\underline{\hat{\bar{b}}}_1 - \underline{\bar{b}}_1) \xrightarrow{P} (\underline{M}_{b_1} - \underline{\bar{b}}_1) \tag{3.16}$$

where $\underline{\hat{\bar{b}}}_1$ is the mixed RCR estimate of $\underline{\bar{b}}_1$; $\underline{\bar{b}}_1$ is the true mean of the distribution of random coefficients; and $\underline{M}_{b_1} = \frac{1}{N} \sum_{i=1}^{N} \underline{b}_{1i}$ is the mean of the 'true' b_{1i}. The notation $\xrightarrow{P}$ means convergence in probability.[1]

Since $(\hat{\underline{b}}_1 - \bar{\underline{b}}_1)$ and $(\underline{M}_{b_1} - \bar{\underline{b}}_1)$ are vectors, we know that convergence in probability will hold for any partition of the vectors.

If we partition as follows

$$\hat{\underline{b}}_1 = \begin{bmatrix} \hat{\underline{\gamma}}_{-1} \\ \hat{\underline{\gamma}}_{-2} \end{bmatrix} \tag{3.17}$$

$$\bar{\underline{b}}_1 = \begin{bmatrix} \bar{\underline{\gamma}}_{-1} \\ \bar{\underline{\gamma}}_{-2} \end{bmatrix} \tag{3.18}$$

and $\underline{M}_{b_1} = \begin{bmatrix} \underline{M}_{\gamma_1} \\ \underline{M}_{\gamma_2} \end{bmatrix}$, $\tag{3.19}$

we can write

$$(\hat{\underline{\gamma}}_1 - \bar{\underline{\gamma}}_1) \xrightarrow{P} (\underline{M}_{\gamma_1} - \bar{\underline{\gamma}}_1). \tag{3.20}$$

Now consider the matrix in equation (C.21):

$$V(\hat{\underline{b}}) = \left[\sum_{j=1}^{N} \left\{ \hat{\underline{\Delta}}_{b_1} + \hat{\sigma}_j^2 (\bar{X}_j' \bar{X}_j)^{-1} \right\}^{-1} \right]^{-1}. \tag{3.21}$$

This is the estimated variance-covariance matrix of the estimator, $\hat{\underline{b}}$, where

$$\hat{\underline{b}} = \begin{bmatrix} \hat{\underline{b}}_1 \\ \hat{\underline{b}}_2 \end{bmatrix}. \tag{3.22}$$

If we now assume that

$$\frac{1}{T}(\bar{X}_j'\bar{X}_j) \xrightarrow{\ P\ } Q_j \ , \tag{3.23}$$

where Q_j is a positive definitive matrix, we can show that

(1) $\quad \hat{\sigma}_j^2 \, (\bar{X}_j'\bar{X}_j)^{-1} = \dfrac{\hat{\sigma}_j^2}{T} \, (\dfrac{1}{T}\bar{X}_j'\bar{X}_j)^{-1}$

$$\xrightarrow{\ P\ } 0, \text{ since } \hat{\sigma}_j^2 \xrightarrow{\ P\ } \sigma_j^2 \text{ , and} \tag{3.24}$$

(2) $\quad \hat{\Delta}_{b_1} = \dfrac{S_{b_1}}{N-1} - \dfrac{1}{N}\sum_{j=1}^{N} \hat{\sigma}_j^2 \, (\bar{X}_j'\bar{X}_j)^{-1}$

$$= \dfrac{S_{b_1}}{N-1} - \dfrac{1}{N}\sum_{j=1}^{N} \dfrac{\hat{\sigma}_j^2}{T} \, (\dfrac{1}{T}\bar{X}_j'\bar{X}_j)^{-1} \tag{3.25}$$

$$\xrightarrow{\ P\ } \dfrac{S_{b_1}}{N-1}$$

where S_{b_1} is defined in equation (C.19) of Appendix C, but using true $\underline{b}_{1i}$ rather than the estimates, $\hat{\underline{b}}_{1i}$. From (3.24) and (3.25) above we have

$$V(\hat{\underline{b}}) \xrightarrow{\ P\ }$$

$$\left[\sum_{j=1}^{N} \left\{\dfrac{S_{b_1}}{N-1}\right\}^{-1}\right]^{-1} = \dfrac{1}{N(N-1)} S_{b_1} \tag{3.26}$$

We now define $V(\hat{\underline{\gamma}}_1)$ to be the $H_1 \times H_1$ partition of $V(\hat{\underline{b}})$ corresponding to the partitioning described in equation (3.2). $V(\hat{\underline{\gamma}}_1)$ is then the estimated covariance matrix of $\hat{\underline{\gamma}}_1$.

Since $V(\hat{\underline{b}}) \xrightarrow{\ P\ } \dfrac{1}{N(N-1)} S_{b_1}$ we know that $V(\hat{\underline{\gamma}}_1)$ will converge in

probability to $\dfrac{1}{N(N-1)} S_{\gamma_1}$ where S_{γ_1} is defined as the upper $H_1 \times H_1$

partition of S_{b_1}. $\dfrac{S_{\gamma_1}}{N-1}$ is the covariance matrix of the "true" γ_{1i}.

By a result in Theil (1971, pp. 361),

$$V(\hat{\hat{\gamma}}_1)^{-1} \xrightarrow{P} N(N-1) S_{\gamma_1}^{-1} \qquad (3.27)$$

Using the results in (3.20) and (3.27) we have

$$|(\hat{\hat{\gamma}}_1 - \bar{\gamma}_1)' V(\hat{\hat{\gamma}}_1)^{-1} (\hat{\hat{\gamma}}_1 - \bar{\gamma}_1) -$$

$$N(N-1) (\underline{M}\gamma_1 - \bar{\gamma}_1)' S_{\gamma_1}^{-1} (\underline{M}\gamma_1 - \bar{\gamma}_1)| \xrightarrow{P} 0 \qquad (3.28)$$

By a theorem in Rao (1973, p. 122) we know that

$$(\hat{\hat{\gamma}}_1 - \bar{\gamma}_1)' V(\hat{\hat{\gamma}}_1)^{-1} (\hat{\hat{\gamma}}_1 - \bar{\gamma}_1) \qquad (3.29)$$

will have the same limiting distribution as

$$N(N-1) (\underline{M}\gamma_1 - \bar{\gamma}_1)' S_{\gamma_1}^{-1} (\underline{M}\gamma_1 - \bar{\gamma}_1). \qquad (3.30)$$

The partition $\dfrac{S_{\gamma_1}}{N-1}$ of $\dfrac{S_{b_1}}{N-1}$ will have a Wishart distribution by a

theorem in Anderson (1958, pp. 162-63). Therefore, as shown in Rao (1973, pp. 541), equation (3.30) has Hotelling's T^2 distribution. Thus, the limiting distribution of equation (3.29) is also Hotelling's T^2. Following the argument in Swamy (1971, pp. 121) and using results from Rao (1973, pp. 541-42) it is easy to show that

$$\dfrac{N-H_1}{H_1(N-1)} \cdot T^2, \qquad (3.31)$$

where

$$T^2 = (\hat{\hat{\gamma}}_1 - \bar{\gamma}_{10})' V(\hat{\hat{\gamma}}_1)^{-1} (\hat{\hat{\gamma}}_1 - \bar{\gamma}_{10}), \qquad (3.32)$$

has, asymptotically, an F-distribution with H_1 and $N\text{-}H_1$ degrees of freedom under the null hypothesis in (3.12).[2]

B. A test of randomness for partitions of the coefficient vector.

In Appendix C we described a statistic for testing randomness of the full random coefficient vector. The test statistic is shown in equation (C.26). Using the likelihood ratio (LR) criterion, we extended this test to a partition of the full vector. However, exact maximum likelihood (ML) estimates were replaced by (computationally feasible) asymptotically equivalent estimates.[3]

The ability of this asymptotic LR statistic to choose the correct specification concerning randomness of coefficients was tested and compared to the ability of an alternative (indirect) test described in the next section. The latter test outperformed the LR test in nearly every case. Results of the simulation used to examine the two tests are presented in Appendix D. Since the LR test did not hold up well in comparison to our alternate test, we have chosen to omit the deriviation of the LR test statistic.

C. Indirect test for randomness of coefficients.

In Appendix C we described a test for equality of coefficient vectors developed by Zellner (1962) and then extended by Swamy (1971, pp. 124-26) to serve as an indirect test for randomness of coefficients. We show here how a similar approach can be used to test for equality of partitions of the random coefficient vector. Details of the derivation are omitted since the general procedures are well known and any extensions of currently available procedures are a matter of algebra.

We again use the model in (3.2):

$$Y_i = Z_{1i} \gamma_{1i} + Z_{2i} \gamma_{2i} + X_{2i}\underline{b}_2 + \underline{e}_i,$$

(3.33)

$$i = 1, \ldots, N.$$

The hypothesis we wish to test is

$$H_o: \gamma_{11} = \gamma_{12} = \cdots \gamma_{1N} = \underline{\gamma}_1 \,(\gamma_1 \text{ not specified})$$

(3.34)

$$\text{vs. } H_a: \gamma_{11} \neq \gamma_{12} \neq \cdots \neq \gamma_{1N} \neq \gamma_1$$

If we reject H_o we are saying that the γ_{1i} differ from one individual unit to another and we have cause to believe these coefficients may be randomly distributed across units. Accepting H_o, on the other hand, means that the coefficients do not vary and, therefore, should not be considered random.

To illustrate a common approach used in deriving an appropriate test statistic we write the model in (3.33) as a full model and a model restricted by the null hypthesis in (3.34).

Full Model:

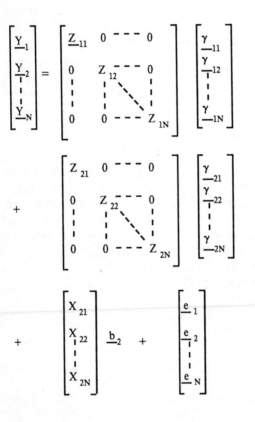

$$(3.35)$$

Restricted Model:

$$
\begin{bmatrix} \underline{Y}_1 \\ \underline{Y}_2 \\ \vdots \\ \underline{Y}_N \end{bmatrix}
=
\begin{bmatrix} Z_{11} \\ Z_{12} \\ \vdots \\ Z_{1N} \end{bmatrix} \underline{\gamma}_1
+
\begin{bmatrix} Z_{21} & 0 & \cdots & 0 \\ 0 & Z_{22} & \cdots & 0 \\ \vdots & & \ddots & \vdots \\ 0 & 0 & \cdots & Z_{2N} \end{bmatrix}
\begin{bmatrix} \underline{\gamma}_{21} \\ \underline{\gamma}_{22} \\ \vdots \\ \underline{\gamma}_{2N} \end{bmatrix}
$$

$$
+
\begin{bmatrix} X_{21} \\ X_{22} \\ \vdots \\ X_{2N} \end{bmatrix} \underline{b}_2
+
\begin{bmatrix} \underline{e}_1 \\ \underline{e}_2 \\ \vdots \\ \underline{e}_N \end{bmatrix}
\tag{3.36}
$$

If we now assume that

$$
E\left\{ \begin{bmatrix} \underline{e}_1 \\ \underline{e}_2 \\ \vdots \\ \underline{e}_N \end{bmatrix} \begin{bmatrix} \underline{e}'_1 & \underline{e}'_2 & \cdots & \underline{e}'_N \end{bmatrix} \right\} = \sigma^2 I
\tag{3.37}
$$

where I is an NT x NT identity matrix we can estimate both these equations by ordinary last squares (see Maddala 1977, pp. 322-26).

To test the hypothesis in (3.34) we can then use

$$
F = \frac{SSE(R)\text{-}SSE(F)}{SSE(F)} \cdot \frac{df(F)}{df(R)\text{-}df(F)} \quad ^{4}
\tag{3.38}
$$

where

SSE(R) and SSE(F) are the residual sums of squares for the restricted and full models respectively and df(R) and df(F) are the associated degrees of freedom. This statistic has an F-distribution with df(R)-df(F) and df(F) degrees of freedom.

From Kendall and Stuart (1969, p. 382) we know that (df(R)-df(F)) · F will tend to a χ^2-distribution with df(R)-df(F) degrees of freedom as the denominator degrees of freedom, df(F), tends to infinity. Thus, in large samples, the statistic $(df(R)-df(F)) \cdot F$ can be viewed as having a χ^2-distribution.

One of Zellner's contributions was to show that, for the full coefficient vector, such an approach is asymptotically equivalent to using the likelihood ratio test statistic, λ, where -2 in λ has a χ^2-distribution with df(R)-df(F) degrees of freedom in large samples.

For the hypothesis in (3.34) Zellner's derivation provides us with the following advantages over the F-statistic in equation (3.38):

(1) We can allow individual variances to differ, i.e., we have the following in place of assumption (3.37):

$$
E\left\{
\begin{bmatrix} \underline{e}_1 \\ \underline{e}_2 \\ \vdots \\ \underline{e}_N \end{bmatrix}
\begin{bmatrix} \underline{e}'_1 & \underline{e}'_2 & \cdots & \underline{e}'_N \end{bmatrix}
\right\}
$$

$$
= \begin{bmatrix}
\sigma_1^2 I & 0 & \cdots & 0 \\
0 & \sigma_2^2 I & & 0 \\
\vdots & \vdots & \ddots & \vdots \\
0 & 0 & \cdots & \sigma_N^2 I
\end{bmatrix}
\tag{3.39}
$$

where the I's are T x T identity matrices and the 0's are T x T matrices of zeros.

(2) We obtain a fairly simple computational form[5] for the statistic:

$$
C = \sum_{i=1}^{N} \left[\frac{(\hat{\underline{Y}}_{1i} - \hat{\underline{Y}}_1)' Z_{1i} \, 'Z_{1i} \, (\hat{\underline{Y}}_{1i} - \hat{\underline{Y}}_1)}{\hat{\sigma}_i^2} \right]
\tag{3.40}
$$

where

C is asymptotically distributed as χ^2 with $(N-1) \cdot H_1$ degrees of freedom;

$\hat{\gamma}_{1i}$ is the OLS estimate of γ_{1i};
$\hat{\gamma}_1$ is the estimate when the N vectors γ_{1i} are considered equal (thus $\hat{\gamma}_1$ is the 'fixed estimate'); and $\hat{\sigma}_i^2$ is the mean square error from the ith regression; and Z_{1i} is defined in equation (3.4).

Little is known of the small sample properties of the test statistics just described. Zellner suggests that using F in equation (3.38) may be more appropriate than using C in equation (3.40) when samples are small. The simulation study summarized in Appendix D, although not exhaustive, provides us with some faith in the χ^2-statistic, C, for samples of size T = 50 or greater.

D. Simultaneous test of the hypothesis that coefficients are both fixed and equal to zero.

As a final extension of the test procedures concerning assumptions about the coefficients in the mixed RCR model we provide a simultaneous test of the hypothesis that a coefficient vector is both (1) fixed and (2) equal to zero.
Again, using our general model we write

$$\underline{Y}_i = Z_{1i}\underline{\gamma}_{1i} + Z_{2i}\ \underline{\gamma}_{2i} + X_{2i}\underline{b}_2 + \underline{e}_i, \qquad (3.41)$$

$$i = 1, \ldots, N.$$

The hypothesis we wish to test is

$$H_o: \ \underline{\gamma}_{11} = \underline{\gamma}_{12} = \ldots = \underline{\gamma}_{1N} = \ \underline{\gamma}_1 = 0$$

vs. $H_a: \ \underline{\gamma}_{11} \neq \underline{\gamma}_{12} \neq \ldots \neq \underline{\gamma}_{1N} \neq \underline{\gamma}_1 = 0.$ \qquad (3.42)

We can immediately note the similarity between this hypothesis and the hypothesis in (3.34) of the previous section. It is the same hypothesis except that we have specified here that $\underline{\gamma}_1$, the value of the fixed coefficient vector if all the γ_{1i} are equal, is equal to zero.
We can modify the statistic in (3.40) to test this simultaneous hypothesis as follows:

$$S = \sum_{i=1}^{N} \frac{\hat{\gamma}_{1i}' Z_{1i}' Z_{1i} \hat{\gamma}_{1i}}{\hat{\sigma}_i^2} .$$ (3.43)

where

$\hat{\gamma}_{1i}$ is the OLS estimate of γ_{1i}, and $\hat{\sigma}_i^2$ is the mean square error from the ith regression.

Under the null hypotheses in (3.42), S will have, asymptotically, the χ^2-distribution with $N \cdot H_1$ degrees of freedom.
As in the previous test this test can be derived using the residual sum of squares from a full and a restricted model and the asymptotic properties of the F-random variable or by using Zellner's LR approach.
We now have the capability to:
(1)   test hypotheses about any portion of the mean vector of random coefficients in the RCR model or mixed RCR model;
(2)   test whether any subset of the coefficients in the RCR or mixed RCR models can be considered random; and
(3)   conduct a simultaneous test of whether a coefficient vector is both fixed and equal to zero.

The importance of such tests for proper model specification should be clear. These tests will play a major role in the schema we will present in Chapter 5.

Section 3.2 Negative Variance Estimates in the Mixed RCR Model.

Negative variance estimates are not a problem unique to Swamy's RCR model. Those familiar with random-effect models in the analysis of variance (ANOVA) will recognize the problem as one that has received much attention. In models represented as

$$y_{it} = \mu + a_i + u_{it}$$ (3.44)

where the a_i's and u_{it}'s are independently distributed random variables we are interested in obtaining estimates of the variances σ_a^2 and σ_u^2. Commonly used techniques to obtain these estimates can lead to negative values of $\hat{\sigma}_a^2$. Suggested remedies for this situation in the ANOVA context are:

1) Set the variance equal to zero whenever a negative estimate is obtained (see Scheffé 1959, p. 229).

2) Use a Bayesian approach with the prior information that variances cannot be negative (see Tiao and Tan, 1965).

3) Use a Bayesian approach with proper prior distributions (see Hill, 1965).

4) Determine whether the model is correctly specified.

Negative variance estimates may occur because of statistical dependence of a_i and a_j ($i \neq j$) or because the u_{it}'s are autocorrelated unless these correlations are taken into account in the estimation techniques (see McHugh and Mielke, 1968 and Tiao and Tan, 1966).

Other work with random coefficient models also highlights this problem. Hildreth and Houck (1968), for example, encounter negative variance estimates when using a random coefficient approach to model a single time series relationship. Their solutions are:

1) Set the variance to zero when negative estimates are obtained; or,

2) Use a restricted estimator subject to the condition that the variances must be non-negative.

Since negative variance estimates have received considerable attention in the literature, we might expect their appearance in using Swamy's RCR approach to present a non-trivial problem with which we must deal. This is highlighted in using a t-statistic to test significance of a fixed coefficient versus using a t-statistic to test significance of the mean of a random coefficient.

The next section will present problems that can be encountered in such tests and will suggest appropriate remedial measures. The discussion will also highlight the importance of correct model specification in terms of the randomness or non-randomness of coefficients.

A. The Use of t-Statistics when
Negative Variance Estimates are Obtained.

Inference in linear models is often concerned with the significance of an individual coefficient. When coefficients are fixed we can test whether or not a coefficient is equal to zero by using the t-statistic constructed as:

$$t_F = \frac{\text{coefficient estimate}}{\text{standard error of the estimate}} \cdot \qquad \text{[6]} \qquad (3.45)$$

Under the null hypothesis that the true coefficient value is zero, this statistic has a t-distribution with NT-K degrees of freedom (K being the number of regression parameters in the model; NT being the number of observations in a classical pooled model).

When coefficients are random our interest might lie in testing whether the mean of the distribution of a coefficient is equal to zero. An asymptotic test based on the t-distribution can again be formulated. In this case

$$t_R = \frac{\text{coefficient mean estimate}}{\text{standard error of the estimate}} . \qquad (3.46)$$

Under the null hypothesis that the coefficient mean is zero t_R will have, asymptotically, the t-distribution with N-1 degrees of freedom.[7]

Suppose we apply this second test to the coefficient b_i, estimated as random, in the simple two variable model

$$y_{it} = b_i X_{it} + e_{it}. \qquad (3.47)$$

Following (3.47) our test statistic is

$$t_R = \frac{\hat{\bar{b}}}{se(\hat{\bar{b}})} . \qquad (3.48)$$

In this section we wish to examine complications which occur when $Var(b_i)$, the population variance of the coefficients b_i, is estimated as being negative. We first present the results for the non-technical reader; in the following section, a more detailed analysis of the situation is presented.

B. Non-Technical Discussion of the Change in the Value of t-Statistics.

Assume that we have completed the estimation process with the model in (3.47). Specifically, we obtain the estimates $\hat{\bar{b}}$, $se(\hat{\bar{b}})$ and $\hat{Var}(b_i)$. The exact procedures for obtaining such estimates can be found in Appendix C in the general case and in part C of this section in the two variable cases. Our interest first centers on the estimate of the population variance of the b_i, $\hat{Var}(b_i)$. The procedure for obtaining this estimate is as follows: Obtain separate equation OLS estimates of the individual b_i

for all N cross-sectional units. Denote these estimates as $\hat{b}_i$. Find the variation in the $\hat{b}_i$ using the formula for sample variance:

$$V(\hat{b}) = \frac{\sum\limits_{i=1}^{N} \hat{b}_i^2 - \dfrac{\left(\sum\limits_{i=1}^{N} \hat{b}_i\right)^2}{N}}{N-1} \tag{3.49}$$

Estimate the sampling variance of each of the $\hat{b}_i$, $V(\hat{b}_i)$, and find the simple average of these values which we denote $\overline{V}(\hat{b}_i)$:

$$\overline{V}(\hat{b}_i) = \frac{1}{N} \sum_{i=1}^{N} V(\hat{b}_i)$$

$$= \frac{1}{N} \sum_{i=1}^{N} \left[\hat{\sigma}_i^2 \left(\sum_{t=1}^{T} x_{it}^2 \right)^{-1} \right]. \tag{3.50}$$

The population variance of the coefficients b_i is then estimated as the difference between $V(\hat{b})$ and $\overline{V}(\hat{b}_i)$:

$$V\hat{a}r(b_i) = V(\hat{b}) - \overline{V}(\hat{b}_i). \tag{3.51}$$

The motivation for such an estimate can be demonstrated by considering the difference $\hat{b}_i - \overline{b}$ and decomposing this difference as

$$\hat{b}_i - \overline{b} = (\hat{b}_i - b_i) + (b_i - \overline{b}). \tag{3.52}$$

Now square both sides of this question, multiply by $\frac{1}{N}$, sum and take expected values to obtain

$$\frac{1}{N} \sum_{i=1}^{N} E(\hat{b}_i - \overline{b})^2 = \frac{1}{N} \sum_{i=1}^{N} E(\hat{b}_i - b_i)^2 + \frac{1}{N} \sum_{i=1}^{N} E(b_i - \overline{b})^2 \tag{3.53}$$

or, by rearranging terms, we can write

$$Var(b_i) = \frac{1}{N} \sum_{i=1}^{N} E(\hat{b}_i - \bar{b})^2 - \frac{1}{N} \sum_{i=1}^{N} E(\hat{b}_i - b_i)^2 \qquad (3.54)$$

$$where \ Var(b_i) = \frac{1}{N} \sum_{i=1}^{N} E(b_i - \bar{b})^2. \qquad (3.55)$$

The term in $\frac{1}{N} \sum_{i=1}^{N} E(\hat{b}_i - \bar{b})^2$ (3.54) can be viewed as the total vari-

ance of the $\hat{b}_i$ around the mean $\bar{b}$. The second term, the average

sampling variance, $\frac{1}{N} \sum_{i=1}^{N} E(\hat{b}_i - b_i)^2$, adjusts for the fact that estimates

of the b_i rather than the true b_i have been used in calculating the
previous variance.

The term $\frac{1}{N} \sum_{i=1}^{N} E(\hat{b}_i - \bar{b})^2$ is estimated using $V(\hat{b})$ of equation

(3.49); $\frac{1}{N} \sum_{i=1}^{N} E(\hat{b}_i - b_i)^2$ is estimated using $\bar{V}(\hat{b}_i)$ of equation (3.50). The

estimate $V\hat{a}r(b_i)$ given in equation (3.51) is an unbiased estimate of $Var(b_i)$.

Since $V\hat{a}r(b_i)$ is the difference of two statistics, there is a possibility
that it will be negative, an undesirable result for a quantity representing
variance. This might occur if the variation in the $\hat{b}_i, V(\hat{b})$ is small
compared to the average sampling variance, $\bar{V}(\hat{b}_i)$. There are instances
when incorrect assumptions concerning residuals can cause such a result.
As pointed out by Swamy (1971, pp. 147-48) the more common instances
where this will occur are:

(1) Assuming the residual variances, σ_i^2 for each individual
regression equation are equal when this assumption is not
appropriate.

(2) Assuming the time series residuals for each individual regression are independent when they are negatively auto-correlated.

(3) Assuming residuals from the same time period but for different individuals are uncorrelated when such contemporaneous correlation does exist.

If we believe the assumptions we have adopted for the residuals in our model are appropriate and we still obtain a negative variance estimate, we would have reason to believe that the coefficient in question is fixed rather than random. We can summarize the above by stating the two possible decisions available when we find $\text{Vâr}(b_i) < 0$.

Decision 1.

The model is incorrectly specified in terms of assumptions concerning the residuals. In this case we test those assumptions to see where incorrect specification might have occurred and re-estimate after corrections are made (Appropriate tests are developed in Chapter 4).

Decision 2.

The coefficients b_i are not random but fixed coefficients. Re-estimate the model using, in this simple two-variable case, a classical pooled regression.

When we decide to take the course of action indicated in Decision 2, our estimate of interest changes from a coefficient mean to that of a fixed coefficient. Use of this approach leads to an interesting, albeit at first glance confusing, result. The following example will illustrate this.

Suppose the estimates in Table 3.1 are obtained for b_i when it is considered random:

Coefficient	Mean	Standard Error	t-statistic	Population Variance
b_i	-.016	.005	-3.4	Negative

Table 3.1 : Estimates for Random Coefficient

Noting the negative estimate of the population variance and believing our residual assumptions to be correct we re-estimate with b_i fixed (i.e., equal to some b for all i) and obtain the results in Table 3.2.

Coefficient	Fixed Estimate	Standard Error	t-statistic
b	.00002	.008	.002

Table 3.2 : Estimates for Fixed Coefficient

Note what has happened to the significance of the coefficient. When considered random the t-statistic for the mean was highly significant. But, when we assume the coefficient is fixed, the t-statistic drops from -3.4 to .002. The fixed coefficient b is not significantly different from zero. As can be seen from the tables, the decrease in absolute value of the t-statistic results from

1) an increase in the standard error (the denominator of the t-statistic)
2) a decrease in absolute value in the parameter estimate (the numerator of the t-statistic)

in moving from the random to the fixed coefficient (example taken from Wright, et al., 1977b).

To emphasize the difference between the estimates of b and $\bar{b}$ we construct a 99% confidence interval for $\bar{b}$ using the information in Table 3..[8]

$$-.016 - 2.58(.005) \leq \bar{b} \leq -.016 + 2.58(.005),$$

$$-.0289 \leq \bar{b} \leq -.0031 \tag{3.56}$$

The estimate of the fixed coefficient is not even contained within this interval.

The change in value of the t-statistic emphasizes the importance of appropriate specification concerning randomness of coefficients. The t-value for the estimated mean gives us the impression that the average response of the dependent variable to the independent variable is significantly different from zero. This impression is faulty, however, if the coefficient is more appropriately viewed as fixed. The importance of the fixed versus random assumption led to an investigation of the change in the t-value. This analytic examination is presented in the following section. The results show that we should expect a change in the value of the t-statistic in moving from a random to a fixed coefficient because of a negative variance estimate. We cannot, however, predict whether the value obtained under the fixed estimation procedure will be greater or less than the value under the random procedure without the introduction of a number of simplifying assumptions.

C. Analytic Treatment of the Change in the Value of t-Statistics.

The t-statistic used to test the hypothesis

$$H_o: \text{parameter} = 0$$

can be written as

$$t = \frac{\text{parameter estimate}}{\text{standard error of the estimate}} . \tag{3.57}$$

We first consider the simplest possible linear regression model having only one explanatory variable,

$$Y_{it} = X_{it} b_i + e_{it} \qquad i = 1, \ldots, N \tag{3.58}$$

and examine the difference in parameter estimates under fixed and random assumptions for b_i.

I. b_i random

Using the results in Appendix C and the notation established in the previous section we know that $\bar{b}$ can be efficiently estimated by

$$\hat{\bar{b}} = \left[\sum_{j=1}^{N} [\hat{V}ar(b_j) + V(\hat{b}_j)]^{-1} \right]^{-1} \sum_{i=1}^{N} [\hat{V}ar(b_i) + V(\hat{b}_i)]^{-1} \hat{b}_i$$

$$\tag{3.59}$$

where $\hat{V}ar(b_i)$ is given by equation (3.51),

$$V(\hat{b}_i) = \hat{\sigma}_i^2 \left(\sum_{t=1}^{T} X_{it}^2 \right)^{-1}, \text{ and} \tag{3.60}$$

$$\hat{b}_i = (\sum_{t=1}^{T} X_{it}^2)^{-1} \sum_{t=1}^{T} X_{it} Y_{it} \tag{3.61}$$

We can simplify the writing of (3.59) further as

$$\hat{\bar{b}} = \sum_{i=1}^{N} W_i \hat{b}_i \tag{3.62}$$

where

$$W_i = \left[\sum_{j=1}^{N} [\hat{Var}(b_j) + V(\hat{b}_j)]^{-1} \right]^{-1} (\hat{Var}(b_i) + V(\hat{b}_i))^{-1} \tag{3.63}$$

Thus $\hat{\bar{b}}$ is a weighted average of the $\hat{b}_i$ with weight W_i given to $\hat{b}_i$.

II. b_i fixed and equal to b for all i.

The fixed estimate of b is obtained using formulat (3.59) assuming that the variance of the b_i, $Var(b_i)$, is zero. We write the estimate as

$$\hat{b} = \sum_{i=1}^{N} W_i^* \hat{b}_i \tag{3.64}$$

where the new weight for $\hat{b}_i$ is

$$W_i^* = \left[\sum_{j=1}^{N} V(\hat{b}_j)^{-1} \right]^{-1} . V(\hat{b}_i)^{-1} \tag{3.65}$$

The values W_i and W_i^* can be viewed as the relative weights given to the OLS coefficient estimates in the cases of random and fixed assumptions respectively. We note that in the random case these weights depend on the estimated variance of the coefficients, $\hat{Var}(b_i)$, as well as the sampling precision, $V(\hat{b}_i)$, of each individual coefficient estimate.

III. Comparison of the standard errors of the estimates $\bar{\hat{b}}$ and $\hat{b}$.

Assume that our residual assumptions are justified and suppose we obtain a negative estimate of the population variance of b_i, i.e., suppose $\hat{Var}(b_i) < 0$.

Then

(1) $\hat{Var}(b_i) + V(\hat{b}_i) < V(\hat{b}_i)$ (3.66)

(2) If $|\hat{Var}(b_i)| < V(\hat{b}_i)$ so that

$\hat{Var}(b_i) + V(\hat{b}_i) > 0$ for all i[9], then

$(\hat{Var}(b_i) + V(\hat{b}_i))^{-1} > V(\hat{b}_i)^{-1}$ (3.67)

(3) $\displaystyle\sum_{i=1}^{N} [\hat{Var}(b_i) + V(\hat{b}_i)]^{-1} > \sum_{i=1}^{N} V(\hat{b}_i)^{-1}$ (3.68)

(4) $\displaystyle\left[\sum_{i=1}^{N} [\hat{Var}(b_i) + V(\hat{b}_i)]^{-1} \right]^{-1} < \left[\sum_{i=1}^{N} V(\hat{b}_i)^{-1} \right]^{-1}$ (3.69)

(5) From Appendix C we know that

$$se(\bar{\hat{b}}) = \left[\sum_{i=1}^{N} [\hat{Var}(b_i) + V(\hat{b}_i)]^{-1} \right]^{-\frac{1}{2}}$$ (3.70)

$$se(\hat{b}) = \left[\sum_{i=1}^{N} V(\hat{b}_i)^{-1} \right]^{-\frac{1}{2}}$$ (3.71)

(6) Using results (4) and (5) we have

$se(\bar{\hat{b}}) < se(\hat{b})$. (3.72)

Thus, when $\mathrm{V\hat{a}r}(b_i) < 0$, it is possible to obtain a smaller standard error of estimate under the assumption that the b_i are random. This is contrary to results when $\mathrm{V\hat{a}r}(b_i) > 0$. In this case we will always have

$$se(\overset{\approx}{b}) > se(\hat{b}).\tag{3.73}$$

Since a result such as (3.72) can lead to inflated values of the t-statistic used to test the significance of a parameter, the course of action in Decision 2 of the previous section is recommended: re-estimate the model with b_i assumed fixed.

IV. Further comparisons

A statement concerning the comparative values of $\overset{\approx}{b}$ and $\hat{b}$ cannot be made as was done for the standard errors. Thus, we know that a change in the value of the t-statistic can be expected in the negative variance case but we cannot make any statement concerning the direction or magnitude of this change.

When two or more explanatory variables are involved, even the standard errors become too complicated to compare analytically. Although the complexity of relationships in this case precludes any clear cut analysis, we should not be surprised to find a change in the value of a t-statistic after setting a negative variance estimate equal to zero.

A further caveat is suggested by these results. In previous sections of this chapter we have been dealing with tests of significance and/or randomness for several coefficients simultaneously. The variance-covariance matrix of those coefficients estimated as random is involved in obtaining the parameter estimates used in these tests. When we obtain a negative estimate for a coefficient variance, this quantity will affect the calculations in these multiple variable tests as well as in the simple one variable test discussed in this section. Thus, a negative variance estimate should again be a warning to (1) test assumptions concerning residuals, and (2) re-specify those coefficients with negative variance estimates as fixed if residual assumptions are satisfied.

A further implication of this discussion pertains to the concept of sequential or stepwise estimation and tests of hypotheses. It is well known that, even in a single equation multiple regression model, when a sequence of tests (say F-tests for coefficient significance) are performed and the regression equation is altered and re-estimated according to these test results, the new parameter estimates and test statistics will lose their original distributional properties unless viewed as values conditional on the previous results. Although no work has been done concerning sequential testing and estimation in the RCR model, we can assume that a similar alteration of distributions will occur after a sequence of tests and model re-specification.

This research will not deal with the development of any such theory. We merely point out that it is a problem to be considered in analyzing data with random coefficient models as well as in the case of any other linear model. When models are developed in such a sequential fashion, our conclusions should be validated on an independent sample.

Chapter 4

Analysis of Model Assumptions
Concerning Disturbances

When using any linear model we make certain assumptions for purposes of estimation and/or inference. Many of these assumptions involve the disturbance terms in the model. This is also the case when our data consists of observations over time on a number of individual units. In order to help us feel confident about the specification of our models of pooled cross-sectional and time series data we may want to test certain of the assumptions made. This chapter will present tests specificially designed for pooled models for testing assumptions made about serial and contemporaneous correlation of disturbances.

Serial correlation is a consideration in nearly all work with time series observations. In our case any serial correlation problems are compounded since we are pooling the observations from several individual time series. The consideration of contemporaneous correlation is suggested by Zellner's (1962) seemingly unrelated regression paper. As he notes, we can obtain parameter estimates that are statistically more efficient if we make use of the additional information concerning contemporaneous correlation in our estimation procedures.

To assess whether either serial or contemporaneous correlation exists, we present the theoretical development of a test for each of these two types of correlation.

Section 4.1 Testing for Serial Correlation

We consider here the market model discussed in Chapter 2 for each of N firms:

$$R_{1t} = a_1 + b_1 R_{mt} + e_{1t}$$

$$R_{2t} = a_2 + b_2 R_{mt} + e_{2t} \tag{4.1}$$

$$\cdot \qquad \cdot$$
$$\cdot \qquad \cdot$$
$$\cdot \qquad \cdot$$

$$R_{Nt} = a_N + b_N R_{mt} + e_{Nt}$$

For each time series regression equation

$$R_{it} = a_i + b_i R_{mt} + e_{it} \tag{4.2}$$

we assume that the disturbances are not serially correlated, i.e.,

$$E(e_{it} e_{it'}) = 0 \text{ for } t \neq t'. \tag{4.3}$$

If this assumption is violated we can improve the specification of our model by modifying the estimation procedures appropriately (see Swamy, 1971, pp. 127-31).

The usual tests performed in regression analysis concern themselves with first-order autocorrelation, i.e., we test to see whether the disturbances follow a first-order autoregressive scheme

$$e_{it} = p_i e_{i,t-1} + u_{it} \tag{4.4}$$

where p_i is the first-order autocorrelation coefficient and the u_{it} meet the assumptions made for ordinary regression disturbance terms. For each individual we test the hypothesis

$$H_o : p_i = 0$$

$$\text{vs } H_a : p_i \neq 0 \tag{4.5}$$

by using the Durbin-Watson statistic (or, alternatively, the von Neumann statistic for large samples: $T > 100$). Since our main concern is with pooled cross-sectional and time series data, we might also be interested in a "global" or "pooled" test for serial correlation. For example, a test of the hypothesis

$$H_o : p_1 = p_2 = \ldots = p_N = p = 0$$

$$\text{vs } H_a : p_1 \neq p_2 \ldots \neq p_N \tag{4.6}$$

with level of significance α.

This is not the same as testing the hypothesis (4.5) with level of significance α for each of the N time series regressions. In (4.6) we want to test simultaneously whether all serial correlation coefficients are zero.[1]

If first-order serial correlation between the time series residuals exists we can write the relationships as follows:

$$e_{it} = p_i e_{i,t-1} + u_{it} \tag{4.7}$$

or, in vector notation, as

$$\underline{e}_i = p_i \underline{e}_i^* + \underline{u}_{it} \tag{4.8}$$

where

$$\underline{e}_i = \begin{bmatrix} e_{i1} \\ e_{i2} \\ | \\ | \\ e_{iT} \end{bmatrix} \quad \text{and} \quad \underline{e}_i^* = \begin{bmatrix} e_{i0} \\ e_{i1} \\ | \\ | \\ e_{iT-1} \end{bmatrix} \tag{4.9}$$

There are two main questions we might ask concerning the auto-correlation coefficients:

(1) Are the p_i equal for all i?
(2) If the p_i are all equal to some value, say p, does p equal zero or does it have a non-zero value?

If $p_1 = p_2 = \ldots = p_n = p = 0$, we know that no problems with serial correlation exist. If the p_i are not all equal or if they are all equal to some value p but $p \neq 0$, then we want to use estimators which allow for the presence of serial correlation.

Methods examined in Chapter 3 and in Appendix C will be adapted here to create methodologies for answering the previous questions. We now present these questions as formal hypotheses and demonstrate how to test these hypotheses.

A. Are the p_i all equal?

The hypothesis to be tested is

$$H_o : p_1 = p_2 = \ldots = p_N = p$$

$$\text{vs } H_a : p_1 \neq p_2 \ldots \neq p_N. \tag{4.10}$$

Writing the first-order autoregressive relationships as in equation (4.8)

$$\underline{e}_i = p_i \underline{e}_i^* + \underline{u}_i \tag{4.11}$$

and assuming we have a large sample, we can apply Zellner's test for equality of coefficients (or for Chow test for coefficient equality) to test the hypothesis in (4.10). Recall that the test developed by Zellner is asymptotically equivalent to the usual F-test applied to full and restricted regression models (i.e., the Chow test), except that the Zellner test allows variances to differ between individual time series regressions.[2] Also, the Zellner test is specificially designed for use with large samples. Concerning the model in equation (4.11) we assume

(1) $\underline{u}_i \sim N(\underline{0}, \sigma_i^2 \, I_T)$

(2) $\underline{e}_i^*$ and $\underline{u}_i$ are independent.

The test statistic can be written

$$R = \sum_{i=1}^{N} \frac{(\hat{p}_i - \hat{p}) \, \underline{e}_i^{*'} \, \underline{e}_i^* \, (\hat{p}_i - \hat{p})}{\hat{\sigma}_i^2} \tag{4.12}$$

$$= \sum_{i=1}^{N} \left[\frac{(\hat{p}_i - \hat{p})^2}{\hat{\sigma}_i^2} \cdot \sum_{t=1}^{T} e_{i,t-1}^2 \right], \tag{4.13}$$

where

$$\hat{p}_i = (\underline{e}_i^{*'} \, \underline{e}_i^*)^{-1} \, \underline{e}_i^{*'} \, \underline{e}_i$$

$$= (\sum_{t=1}^{T} e_{i,t-1}^2)^{-1} \sum_{t=1}^{T} e_{i,t-1} \, e_{it} \tag{4.14}$$

is the separate equation OLS estimate of the ith autocorrelation coefficient,

$$\hat{p} = \left[\sum_{i=1}^{N} (\underline{e}_i^{*'} \, \underline{e}_i^*) \right]^{-1} \sum_{i=1}^{N} \underline{e}_i^{*'} \, \underline{e}_i \tag{4.15}$$

is the classical pooled estimate of p, the fixed value of the autocorrelation coefficient under the null hypothesis in (4.10),

$$\hat{\sigma}_i^2 = \frac{\hat{\underline{u}}_i' \, \hat{\underline{u}}_i}{T-1} \tag{4.16}$$

is the mean error from the ith separate equation regression of $\underline{e}_i$ on $\underline{e}_i^*$, and $\hat{\underline{u}}_i$ is the estimated residual vector from such a regression:

$$\hat{\underline{u}}_i = \underline{e}_i - \hat{p}_i \underline{e}_i^*. \tag{4.17}$$

Under H_0, R is asymptotically distributed as χ^2 with N-1 degrees of freedom.

B. Are the p_i all equal to zero?

The hypothesis of interest is

$$H_o : p_1 = p_2 = \ldots = p_N = p = 0$$

$$\text{vs } H_a : p_1 \neq \ldots \neq p_N \tag{4.18}$$

This is the simultaneous test that coefficients are all equal to zero. The test statistic is developed from R in the previous section by assuming p (and thus $\hat{p}$) is equal to zero.

The new statistic for testing the hypothesis in (4.18) is

$$RE = \sum_{i=1}^{N} \left[\frac{\hat{p}_i^2}{\hat{\sigma}_i^2} \sum_{t=1}^{T} e^2_{i,t-1} \right]. \tag{4.19}$$

Under H_o, RE is asymptotically distributed as χ^2 with N degrees of freedom.[3]

The hypothesis in (4.18) is of great importance in deciding whether serial correlation is a problem of any significance in our model. If the null hypothesis in (4.18) is accepted, we conclude that first order serial correlation exists for at least one of the time series regressions. At this point we might conduct the test in Part A. Acceptance of H_o in (4.10) will tell us that the first-order serial correlation coefficients for each of the N separate equation residuals are equal and will provide us with the value of the pooled correlation coefficient, $\hat{p}$, in equation (4.15). If the null hypothesis in (4.10) is also rejected, we must conclude that the serial correlation coefficients differ and that at least one is non-zero.

The approach taken to remedy the problem of serial correlation is the same whether we are estimating separate equation OLS regressions or whether we plan to do a pooled analysis using, say, SUR or RCR. We estimate p_i (or p if the null hypothesis in (4.10) is accepted) and use this estimate, $\hat{p}_i$, to transform the data in order to produce a series with noncorrelated residuals. We then re-estimate using the new series. This procedure is well known and is outlined in most elementary econometrics texts (see Pindyck and Rubinfeld, 1976, pp. 108-11 or Theil, 1971, pp. 250-54).

The problem we encounter in using the test statistics presented in equations (4.13) or (4.19) is that the true residuals, the e_{it}, are unknown (and unobservable). Therefore, in order to apply these tests in practice, we must find suitable substitutes for the e_{it}. Our substitutes will be the OLS residuals obtained by regressing R_{it} on R_{mt} for each of the N firms. Performing these N time series regressions we use the estimated residual

$$\hat{e}_{it} = R_{it} - \hat{a}_i - \hat{b}_i R_{mt}.$$
(4.20)

where $\hat{a}_i$ and $\hat{b}_i$ are the OLS estimates of a_i and b_i, to replace the actual residual

$$e_{it} = R_{it} - a_i - b_i R_{mt} .$$
(4.21)

This approach is justified asymptotically. We know from Theil (1971, pp. 378-79) that

$$\hat{e}_{it} - e_{it} \xrightarrow{P} 0$$
(4.22)

as $T \rightarrow \infty$.

Therefore in large samples the estimated residual, $\hat{e}_{it}$, should provide a good approximation of the true residual, e_{it}. Again, the effectiveness of tests based on such asymptotic theory remains to be seen when applied in small samples.

Now that we have obtained the $\hat{e}_{it}$ we can use this data to estimate the p_i.

The vectors $\underline{\hat{e}}_i$ and $\underline{\hat{e}}_i{}^*$, where

$$\underline{\hat{e}}_i = \begin{bmatrix} \hat{e}_{i2} \\ \hat{e}_{i3} \\ \vdots \\ \hat{e}_{iT} \end{bmatrix} \quad \text{and} \quad \underline{\hat{e}}_i{}^* = \begin{bmatrix} \hat{e}_{i1} \\ \hat{e}_{i2} \\ \vdots \\ \hat{e}_{iT-1} \end{bmatrix}$$
(4.23)

are substituted for $\underline{e}_i$ and $\underline{e}_i{}^*$ in equation (4.11). We then perform the regressions

$$\underline{\hat{e}}_i = p_i \underline{\hat{e}}_i{}^* + \underline{u}_i{}^4.$$
(4.24)

Note that we have lost one of our true residuals since we do not estimate e_{io} of equation (4.9). Again, the loss of this observation is inconsequential asymptotically.

Using the $\hat{p}_i$ obtained from the regressions performed in (4.24) we can construct test statistics such as R and RE to determine whether there is significant serial correlation in our model. The property (4.22) insures us that the statistics R and RE calculated using the $\hat{e}_{it}$ will have the same distributions asymptotically as if we used the true e_{it}.

Section 4.2 Testing for Contemporaneous Correlation

Consider again the market model for a cross-section of N firms:

$$R_{1t} = a_1 + b_1 R_{mt} + e_{1t}$$

$$R_{2t} = a_2 + b_2 R_{mt} + e_{2t}$$

.   .
.   .
.   .
.   .
.   .

$$R_{Nt} = a_N + b_N R_{mt} + e_{Nt} \qquad (4.25)$$

A second assumption made in most pooled analyses is that correlation of the disturbance terms between cross-sectional units does not exist, i.e.,

$$E(e_{it}\, e_{jt}) = 0 \text{ for } i \neq j. \qquad (4.26)$$

This type of correlation, called contemporaneous correlation, may be present in certain cases. For example, in the equations in (4.25) we are using the variable R_{mt} to remove any systematic component in the time series of returns. Perhaps there is a systematic behavior for the firms involved with respect to certain industry groups. If this were so, we might expect the residuals in time period t for firms in the same industry to be correlated. Thus we would have

$$E\, (e_{it}\, e_{jt}) = \sigma_{ij} \neq 0 \qquad (4.27)$$

for at least some $i \neq j$.

In this section we propose a test for such contemporaneous correlation.

For the construction of this test we view the equation system in (4.25) as having been written for a fixed value of t. We then define the vector

$$\underline{e}_t = \begin{bmatrix} e_{1t} \\ e_{2t} \\ \vdots \\ e_{Nt} \end{bmatrix} \tag{4.28}$$

where is it assumed that $\underline{e}_t$ is a random variable with a multivariate normal distribution having mean $\underline{0}$ and covariance matrix Σ,

$$\underline{e}_t \sim N(\underline{0}, \Sigma). \tag{4.29}$$

We have thus partitioned the vector $\underline{e}_t$ of (4.28) into N variates or components representing the residuals for a fixed value of t for each of the N cross-sectional units. We want to test the independence of these N variates using a sample of T observation vectors from the population in equation (4.29). Accordingly, the matrix Σ is partitioned into its scalar components:

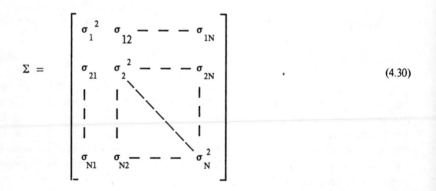

$$\Sigma = \begin{bmatrix} \sigma_1^2 & \sigma_{12} & - & - & - & \sigma_{1N} \\ \sigma_{21} & \sigma_2^2 & - & - & - & \sigma_{2N} \\ \vdots & \vdots & & \ddots & & \vdots \\ \sigma_{N1} & \sigma_{N2} & - & - & - & \sigma_N^2 \end{bmatrix}, \tag{4.30}$$

where σ_{ij} is the covariance between the residuals at time t for firms i and j:

$$\sigma_{ij} = E(e_{it}\,e_{jt}), \tag{4.31}$$

for $i \neq j$.

Hypotheses for the test of independence can be written as follows:

$$H_0 : \Sigma = \Sigma_0 = \begin{bmatrix} \sigma_1^2 & 0 & - & - & - & 0 \\ 0 & \sigma_2^2 & - & - & - & 0 \\ | & | & & \ddots & & | \\ | & | & & & \ddots & | \\ | & | & & & & \ddots \\ 0 & 0 & - & - & - & \sigma_N^2 \end{bmatrix} \qquad (4.32)$$

or $\sigma_{ij} = 0$ for all $i \neq j$.

The null hypothesis in (4.32) states that all covariances are zero but allows for heteroscedasticity of residuals between firms. The alternative hypothesis which follows allows the covariances to be non-zero:

$$H_a : \Sigma = \Sigma_a = \begin{bmatrix} \sigma_1^2 & \sigma_{12} & - & - & - & \sigma_{1N} \\ \sigma_{21} & \sigma_2^2 & - & - & - & \sigma_{2N} \\ | & | & & \ddots & & | \\ | & | & & & \ddots & | \\ | & | & & & & \sigma^2 \\ \sigma_{N1} & \sigma_{N2} & - & - & - & \sigma_N^2 \end{bmatrix} \qquad (4.33)$$

We now use the likelihood ratio criterion in constructing the test statistic. The previous partitioning of matrices and vectors as well as the construction of the test statistic closely follows Anderson's (1958, pp. 230-46) presentation of a multivariate test of independence for sets of variates.

Suppose we can observe a sample of size T independent observation vectors from the N $(\underline{0}, \Sigma)$ population discussed previously. Denote this sample as

$\underline{e}_1, \underline{e}_2, \ldots, \underline{e}_T$.

The likelihood function under H_o given this sample is

$$L(\Sigma_o \,|\, \underline{e}_1, \ldots, \underline{e}_T) = \prod_{t=1}^{T} (2\pi)^{-\frac{N}{2}} \,|\Sigma_o|^{-\frac{1}{2}} \exp\left\{ -\frac{1}{2} \underline{e}_t' \Sigma_o^{-1} \underline{e}_t \right\} \tag{4.34}$$

$$= (2\pi)^{-\frac{NT}{2}} \prod_{i=1}^{N} \sigma_i^{-T} \exp\left\{ -\frac{1}{2} \sum_{t=1}^{T} \underline{e}_t' \Sigma_o^{-1} \underline{e}_t \right\}$$

The likelihood under H_a is

$$L(\Sigma_a \,|\, \underline{e}_1, \ldots, \underline{e}_T) = \prod_{t=1}^{T} (2\pi)^{-\frac{N}{2}} \,|\Sigma_a|^{-\frac{1}{2}} \exp\left\{ -\frac{1}{2} \underline{e}_t' \Sigma_a^{-1} \underline{e}_t \right\} \tag{4.35}$$

$$= (2\pi)^{-\frac{NT}{2}} \,|\Sigma_a|^{-\frac{T}{2}} \exp\left\{ -\frac{1}{2} \sum_{t=1}^{T} \underline{e}_t' \Sigma_a^{-1} \underline{e}_t \right\}$$

Maximizing $L(\Sigma_o| \, \underline{e}_1, \ldots, \underline{e}_T)$ and $L(\Sigma_a| \, \underline{e}_1, \ldots, \underline{e}_T)$ we obtain

$$\sup_{\Sigma_o} L_o (\Sigma_o \,|\, \underline{e}_1, \ldots, \underline{e}_T) = \tag{4.36}$$

$$(2\pi)^{-\frac{NT}{2}} \prod_{i=1}^{N} \hat{\sigma}_i^{-T} \exp\left\{ -\frac{NT}{2} \right\}$$

$$\sup_{\Sigma_a} L_a (\Sigma_a \,|\, \underline{e}_1, \ldots, \underline{e}_T) = \tag{4.37}$$

$$(2\pi)^{-\frac{NT}{2}} \,|\hat{\Sigma}_a|^{-\frac{T}{2}} \exp\left\{ -\frac{NT}{2} \right\}$$

where

$$\hat{\sigma}_i^2 = \frac{1}{T} \sum_{t=1}^{T} e_{it}^2 \tag{4.38}$$

$$\hat{\Sigma}_a = \frac{1}{T} \sum_{t=1}^{T} \underline{e}_t \, \underline{e}_t' \tag{4.39}$$

The likelihood ratio criterion is

$$\lambda = \frac{\displaystyle\sup_{\Sigma_o} L(\Sigma_o | \underline{e}_1, \ldots, \underline{e}_T)}{\displaystyle\sup_{\Sigma_a} L(\Sigma_a | \underline{e}_1, \ldots, \underline{e}_T)} =$$

$$\frac{|\hat{\Sigma}_a|^{T/2}}{\displaystyle\prod_{i=1}^{N} \hat{\sigma}_i^{T}} = \frac{\left| \displaystyle\sum_{t=1}^{T} \underline{e}_t \, \underline{e}_t' \right|^{T/2}}{\left[\displaystyle\prod_{i=1}^{N} \left(\displaystyle\sum_{t=1}^{T} e_{it}^2 \right) \right]^{T/2}} \; . \tag{4.40}$$

$-2 \ln \lambda$ is distributed asymptotically as $\chi^2 \, (\tfrac{1}{2}N(N+1))$.

Of course we don't know the true values of the e_{it}. Therefore some alternative approach must be taken before the use of λ is feasible in practice.

Suppose we perform N separate equation time series regressions and obtain the OLS residuals from each of the regressions:

$$\hat{e}_{it} = R_{it} - \hat{a}_i - \hat{b}_i R_{mt}. \tag{4.41}$$

We would like to use these estimated residuals in place of the true residuals in the test statistic in equation (4.40), but there are problems encountered in such an approach. The least squares residuals will not provide us with an independent sample as we assumed was available in the construction of λ. Also, the asymptotic distribution of $-2\ln\lambda$ was derived under the assumption that we use the true e_{it} rather than estimates of the e_{it}.

We do know, however, that the OLS residuals converge to the true residuals (see Theil, 1971, pp. 378–79):

$$\hat{e}_{it} - e_{it} \xrightarrow{P} 0 \text{ as } T \rightarrow \infty. \tag{4.42}$$

Thus if our sample size, T, is large, we can justify substituting the

OLS residuals for the true residuals in equation (4.40) on the basis of asymptotic properties. We write

$$
\hat{\lambda} = \frac{\left| \sum_{t=1}^{T} \hat{\underline{e}}_t \, \hat{\underline{e}}_t' \right|^{T/2}}{\left[\prod_{i=1}^{N} \left(\sum_{t=1}^{T} \hat{e}_{it}^2 \right) \right]^{T/2}}
\tag{4.43}
$$

Since the $\hat{e}_{it}$ converge in probability to the e_{it} we know that $\hat{\lambda}$ will converge in probability to λ . Thus, by a theorem in Rao (1973, pp. 122), $-2\ln\lambda$ and $-2\ln\hat{\lambda}$ have the same limiting distribution so that $-2\ln\hat{\lambda}$ is asymptotically distributed as χ^2 ($\frac{1}{2}N(N + 1)$). Again, the use of this test is only justified in large samples since its small properties are unknown.

Chapter 5

A General Schema for Analyzing
Pooled Cross-Sectional and Time Series Data

In Chapter 2 we presented a number of techniques for analyzing pooled cross-sectional and time series data. Although the approach taken was one of analyzing financial market data, the pooling methods have general applicability in many different fields. When the empirical data analyst is faced with such a plethora of techniques, he may find himself at a loss in choosing a method appropriate for his particular data. There are several alternatives open at this initial point in the analysis. The different models presented in Chapter 2 are summarized below to emphasize these alternatives:

1. Separate Equation Regressions

This analysis treats each cross-sectional unit individually and estimates a separate time series regression equation for each unit.

2. Seemingly Unrelated Regressions

We again treat the cross-sectional units separately but now use additional information provided by a common disturbance structure to achieve greater efficiency in our parameter estimates. See Zellner (1962) or Kmenta (1971, pp. 517-29).

3. Aggregation of Relations

We transform a number of individual relations to a relation for the group as a whole. One can then perform a single OLS time series regression to estimate the parameters (which must be equal for all individual units or we have a specification error). See Theil (1971, pp. 556-62).

4. Classical Pooling

Analyze all data available in a single "pooled" regression. This method assumes that regression coefficients are equal for all units. See Pindyck and Rubinfeld (1976, pp. 202-3).

5. Analysis of Covariance (ANCOVA)

Covariance analysis, sometimes called least squares with dummy variables (LSDV) when used with time series data over a number of cross-sectional units, allows the intercept of a classical pooled regression equation to vary from one cross-sectional unit to another. If we agree that the intercepts may differ for each cross-sectional unit, then we estimate a parameter (the coefficient of a dummy variable) which reflects this difference for each unit. For technical details, see Brownlee (1965, pp. 376-90).

6. Error Components Model

This model again allows the intercept to vary while assuming the other coefficients are the same for all units. The variation is approached in a different manner than was done with the ANCOVA approach. We treat the intercept as a random variable which varies over cross-sectional units. Using the error components approach we would be concerned with the distribution of the random intercept rather than actual parameter estimates. We attempt to describe this distribution by estimating certain population parameters; then we adjust the coefficient estimates for the effect of the intercept. See Pindyck and Rubinfeld (1976, pp. 206-8) for a brief presentation or Nerlove (1971a) for more detail.

7. Random Coefficient Regression (RCR) Models

The RCR model treats all coefficients as random variables. Thus we allow variation not only in the intercept but in the slope coefficients. Again, the usual attempt to describe this variation is by estimating the population mean and variance of the distribution of each coefficient. See Swamy (1970), (1971, pp. 97-142), or (1974, pp. 143-68).

8. Mixed RCR Models

As a special case of the RCR model, the mixed RCR model allows us to view certain of the coefficients as random from one cross-sectional unit to another and certain of the coefficients as fixed (equal) for all units. See Swamy (1971, pp. 143-55) or Appendix C.

When a researcher is familiar with his particular discipline but is inexperienced in dealing with time series observations on a number of cross-sectional units, he may find the task of choosing a particular method of analysis bewildering. As the use of these pooled data structures becomes more common, the need for a structured approach to the choice of a particular model is evident. In this chapter an initial attempt is made to provide such structure through the presentation of a schema for the analysis of pooled cross-sectional and time series data. This schema will involve a number of basic questions the researcher will need to ask himself. The answers to these questions should lead to the method most appropriate for the analysis of his data.

The approach to be taken in our schema wil be one we might appropriately term an "interactive statistical analysis." In choosing a model we suggest the following techniques characteristic of an interactive approach:

(1) Specification and estimation of linear regression models involving various carefully chosen explanatory variables.
(2) Selecting between alternative models using appropriately formulated hypothesis tests (along with other considerations).
(3) Graphical examination of the regression models and their underlying data.

The schema is broken down into three major sections:

Section 5.1:   Model Selection
Section 5.2:   Testing of Assumptions, and
Section 5.3:   Variable Choice.

The schema will be presented in the above order for expository convenience although this is not necessarily the order in which one would proceed in practice. For example, the first task of the researcher is, of course, to recognize what it is that interests him. This is reflected in his choice of dependent and independent variables by specifying relationships to be examined and tested. Thus the initial choice of variables must be made at the first stage of the process. After selecting an appropriate model, the researcher may use hypothesis testing procedures to delete certain of these original variables or to add other variables not included in the original set. Variable choice, therefore, may take place as the first step in the analysis and as a later step as well.

Section 5.1 Model Selection

In choosing a model for data which occurs as time series observations on a number of individual units the first consideration of the schema is whether coefficient estimates for each individual unit are needed or whether it is the overall effect across all firms that is of interest. For example, one may be interested in the response of an individual firm's rate of return to a previous stock repurchase announcement in contemplating a future repurchase. Or we may want to determine how increases in advertising expense have affected sales for each member of a chain of stores. In each instance it is the individual coefficient estimate for each cross-sectional unit that is of interest.

On the other hand, our concern may lie in the overall or market effect of repurchase announcements on rates of return or in the overall effect of advertising on sales for a population of firms. We no longer have a desire to investigate the behavior of a particular firm; rather, we want to say something about the overall effect on the population of firms. Perhaps we believe there is some population mean effect of advertising on sales and we want to determine whether this effect is positive. Using a sample of firms we will want to somehow estimate the mean effect and use this estimate to make an inference about the population mean.

Appropriate techniques differ according to whether we want individual coefficient estimates or estimates of the overall effect of a variable in our linear model. As we progress through the steps in the schema, options will be illustrated by diagrams similar to a flowchart. The first option is shown in Figure 5.1.

We first assume that option B has been chosen, i.e., we want to examine the effects on each individual firm of a particular variable(s). The next step is to ask whether coefficient estimates for the variable or variables in our model differ from one firm to another. Does advertising expense or a repurchase announcement affect each firm in exactly the same way or does the effect differ in a manner we have not yet explained? As shown in Figure 5.2, if the coefficients differ we have reached the end of one of our flowchart branches. We can use separate regressions to estimate the coefficients for each firm, or, if residuals are correlated between firms, we can use the seemingly unrelated regression approach of Zellner.

FIGURE 5.1
ARE WE INTERESTED IN OBTAINING COEFFICIENT
ESTIMATES FOR EACH INDIVIDUAL UNIT OR IN
MEASURING OVERALL OR 'MEAN' EFFECTS?

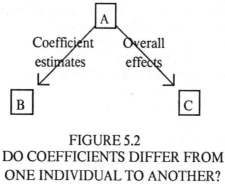

FIGURE 5.2
DO COEFFICIENTS DIFFER FROM
ONE INDIVIDUAL TO ANOTHER?

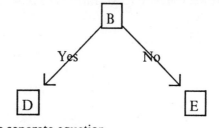

Use separate equation
regressions or SUR

If the responses do not differ from one firm to another, we again have a decision to make. We ask at this point whether the intercepts differ.

If the intercepts as well as the coefficients are the same for all cross-sectional units, appropriate techniques for modeling the relationship are classical pooling or aggregation. Use of aggregation over individual units will not result in the aggregation bias discussed by Theil (1971, pp. 556-62).

If the intercepts differ while the slope coefficients do not, we can ask whether the intercept estimates are of interest specifically or whether they provide no useful information. See Figure 5.3.

Analysis of covariance provides us with an estimate of the change in cross-section intercepts with respect to the first individual unit if such estimates are desired. The desire for these estimates occurs more frequently in the design of experiments where the "covariates" or variables in the regression equation are used to adjust the estimates of the intercepts. It is the intercepts in which we are primarily interested, however. In many business and economic applications we are willing to ignore the intercept estimates since the information they provide is minimal. The error components model reverses the approach of ANCOVA by treating the intercept as a random variable with the value for individual firms viewed as being drawn from a population described by a mean and variance. The mean and variance are then estimated and used to adjust the coefficient estimates. Since the number of parameters to estimate is considerably reduced by the error components approach, its use should be considered when the intercepts add little or no information to an analysis.

FIGURE 5.3
DO INTERCEPTS DIFFER?
(ARE THERE INDIVIDUAL EFFECTS INVOLVED?)

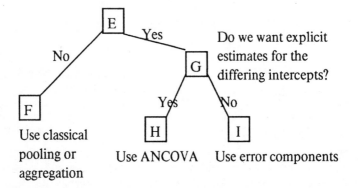

To aid in making decisions about whether coefficients differ from one individual unit to another, the researcher has at his disposal several possible statistical techniques.

Maddala (1977, pp. 322-26) summarizes several statistical tests to determine the appropriate degree of pooling. These tests will take the general form

$$F = \frac{(SSE(R) - SSE(F))/(df(R) - df(F))}{SSE(F)/df(F)} \tag{5.1}$$

where

$$SSE(R) = \text{the restricted residual sum of squares}$$
$$SSE(F) = \text{the full residual sum of squares}$$
$$df(R) = \text{the number of degrees of freedom associated with the restricted sum of squares}$$
$$df(F) = \text{the number of degrees of freedom associated with the full sum of squares}$$

For example, suppose we postulate a regression equation of the form

$$Y_{it} = a_i + b_i X_{it} + e_{it} \quad \begin{matrix} i = 1, \ldots, N \\ t = 1, \ldots, T \end{matrix} \tag{5.2}$$

for the ith individual unit. We want to know whether the slopes and intercepts for each of our N individuals are the same so that we can pool all of our N·T observations into a single regression. The null hypothesis we wish to test is

$$H_0: a_1 = a_2 = \ldots = a_N \text{ and}$$

$$b_1 = b_2 = \ldots = b_N. \tag{5.3}$$

To perform this test we need to know the residual sum of squares from each separate regression. Denote these by SSE_i so that the full sum of squares becomes

$$SSE(F) = \sum_{i=1}^{N} SSE_i . \tag{5.4}$$

We also need the residual sum of squares from the classical pooled regression, SSE(R).

We are using N·T observations to estimate 2N parameters in the unrestricted case. Thus SSE(F) has NT - 2N degrees of freedom. In the poled regression there are only two parameters of estimate so we have NT-2 degrees of freedom. We can now construct our F-statistic:

$$F = \frac{(SSE(R) - SSE(F))/(2N - 2)}{SSE(F)/(NT - 2N)} . \tag{5.5}$$

Under H_o, F as the F distribution with 2N-2 and NT-2N degrees of freedom.

This approach can also be used to test hypotheses concerning only the intercepts or only the slopes. If we have a multiple regression we can also formulate a test that concerns only the equality of a portion of the coefficient vectors.

An alternative approach to test for coefficient equality is discussed in Appendix C. This test was originally developed by Zellner (1962) for the full vector of coefficients. Extension to partitions of the coefficient vector is discussed in Chapter 3. It should be pointed out that (df(R) - df(F)) · F, where F is the statistic in (5.1) and that the chi-square statistic, C, of equation (3.43) in Chapter 3 are asymptotically equivalent.[1] The degrees of freedom, df(R) - df(F), of the chi-square statistic does not involve T since the test is constructed assuming T is a very large (T → ∞). Also, the chi-square statistic easily allows for variances which differ between cross-sectional units in the calculation of SSE(R). This can be done with the F-statistic of (5.1) but is an option which is usually neglected in most readily available regression routines.

Wallace (1972, pp. 689-98) suggests an alternative to the F-test approach just discussed. He shows that, even though coefficients may differ between individual units, the variance obtained from estimating them as equal is smaller than the individual estimator variances. But the pooled estimates will, as pointed out in Theil (1971, pp. 556-62), be biased. Wallace suggests that we may be willing to make a trade-off in certain cases, accepting some bias in order to reduce variances. Accordingly, he develops a test based on mean squared error (MSE)[2] using the same F-statistic as in (5.1). The comparison is not made with tabulated central F distribution values but with non-central F values. These values have been calculated and are presented in a paper by Goodnight and Wallace (1972, pp. 699-709).

We have exhausted the alternatives at this point when individual coefficient estimates are desired and turn to the second branch in Figure 5.1. We want to determine the overall effect or mean effect of an independent variable on our dependent variable. Our first question is the same as in the case previously examined: Do coefficients differ from one cross-sectional unit to another? See Figure 5.4.

To help answer this question we can use the F-tests or the chi-square test previously discussed.

If our test results tell us that the regression coefficients are the same for all individual units we have reached point K in Figure 5.5. We may at this point conduct one final test in order to decide upon our method of analysis. Using an appropriate test we determine whether the intercepts are equal for all our individual units. If not we will use the error components model since we know that individual intercept

estimates are unnecessary.   If the intercepts as well as the slope
coefficients are equal, the appropriate method for analysis is either
classical pooling or aggregation.

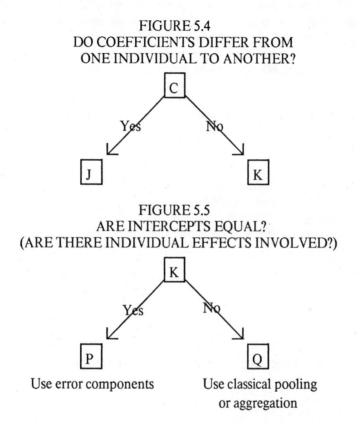

FIGURE 5.4
DO COEFFICIENTS DIFFER FROM
ONE INDIVIDUAL TO ANOTHER?

Yes   No

J   K

FIGURE 5.5
ARE INTERCEPTS EQUAL?
(ARE THERE INDIVIDUAL EFFECTS INVOLVED?)

Yes   No

P   Q

Use error components   Use classical pooling
or aggregation

        If regression coefficients differ between individual cross-sectional
units, we have reached decision point J in Figure 5.6.   At this point the
researcher is left to answer a question without the aid of statistical tests.
He is interested in overall or mean effects and he knows that coefficients
differ between individual units.   Can these coefficients be viewed as
random between units?   There is no test to help us determine whether
coefficients should be viewed as fixed but different as opposed to
random.   If we should choose the concept of fixed but different
coefficients we must again resort to separate equation regressions as our
technique of analysis.   To determine overall effects we must then find
some average of the coefficient estimates and decide whether this average
is significantly different from zero as suggested in Appendix A.

If random coefficient techniques are viewed as a viable alternative, we can move away from the separate equation modeling approach to a more coherent pooled analysis. At decision point L we then ask whether all coefficients should be viewed as random or whether some are more appropriately viewed as fixed placing us in the mixed RCR framework. There are statistical tests available to help in this decision when random coefficient techniques are to be considered. These are illustrated in Swamy (1971, pp. 149-55) and extended in Chapter 3.

FIGURE 5.6
CAN COEFFICIENTS BE VIEWED AS RANDOM?

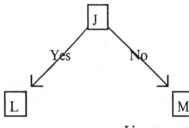

Use separate regressions
or SUR (back to the
old days)

FIGURE 5.7
ARE ALL COEFFICIENTS RANDOM?

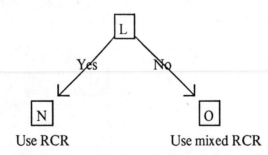

In Figure 5.8, the complete flowchart of decision points is illustrated. This flowchart is not intended to be the final word in analyzing pooled cross-sectional and time series data. The individual researcher may want to append the chart according to the needs of his own discipline. Also, the chart may be altered as analytical research

FIGURE 5.8
COMPLETE FLOWCHART

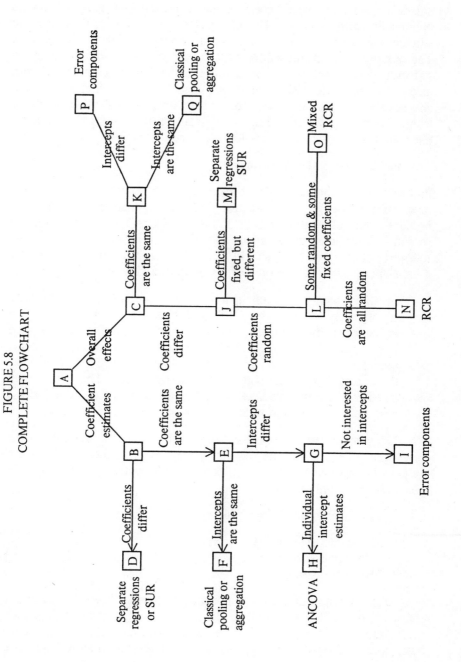

continues on new methods of analysis. For example, this research did not deal with time varying coefficients. Thus, the flowchart includes no options for such models. The incorporation of these models into the schema would provide a possibly useful extension for some future date. The schema was purposefully kept brief and somewhat lacking in statistical detail since its aim is to provide the empirical researcher with ideas concerning the basic techniques for analyzing pooled cross-sectional and time series data and ideas concerning when the use of each of the techniques is appropriate. For more detail on the tests and techniques the reader is referred to the articles referenced throughout this work.

Section 5.2 Testing of Assumptions

Part one of the schema involves the decision as to which type of model is most appropriate for the particular data to be analyzed. Beyond or perhaps even before this problem is the determination of the validity of certain assumptions made about the residuals in our models. The following quote from Maddala (1977, p. 332) may help to give the reader a better perspective on the problem to be discussed here:

> In all problems of pooling, it is first important to estimate each equation individually by OLS and check whether there is any systematic behavior in the slope and intercept coefficients. If there is a systematic pattern in the intercepts, the variance-components model is appropriate. In addition, we should also study whether there is a systematic pattern in the residuals. This will reveal whether the residuals are autocorrelated and/or correlated across cross-section units and what model is appropriate.

His comments on systematic behavior of intercepts and coefficients have already been taken into account in Section 5.1 of the schema. Here we examine systematic behavior of the residuals in terms of assumptions which are commonly made.

Typical assumptions concerning residuals include:

(1) No contemporaneous correlation,
(2) No serial correlation,
(3) Normal distributions.

Our discussion of these assumptions has thus far been limited to the consideration of Zellner's SUR model. The use of this model improves the efficiency of parameter estimates when residuals are contemporaneously correlated. In certain applications, the researcher may feel that one or more of the above conditions needs to be tested before analyzing the data any further.

The tests from Chapter 4 were developed specifically for use with pooled cross-sectional and time series data to test for autocorrelation and contemporaneous correlation. The tests are asymptotically justified but little is known about their small sample properties. The researcher should therefore be cautioned if the size of his sample (the time series length, T) is small.

The Chapter 4 tests include:

(1) A test of the hypothesis that the serial correlation coefficients, p_i, for each our N time series are equal.

   The statistic R in equation (4.13) is used to test this hypothesis.   Under the hypothesis that serial correlation coefficients are all equal, R has a chi-square distribution with N-1 degrees of freedom.

(2) A test of the hypothesis that the N serial correlation coefficients are all equal to zero.

   The statistic RE in equation (4.19) is used in this case and will have a chi-square distribution with N degrees of freedom when all serial correlation coefficients are zero.

(3) A test of the hypothesis that no contemporaneous correlation is present.

   The test statistic, $\hat{\lambda}$, of equation (4.43) is used. Under the null hypothesis of no contemporaneous correlation, -2 times the natural logarithm of $\hat{\lambda}$, $-2\ln\hat{\lambda}$, will have a chi-square distribution with $\frac{1}{2}N(N+1)$ degrees of freedom; N is the number of cross-sectional units in our sample.

If tests indicate that residuals are either autocorrelated or contemporaneously correlated, estimation techniques should be used which take into account the correlation of the residuals thus providing more efficient parameter estimates. See Johnston (1972), pp. 259-65, Zellner (1962) and Swamy (1974), pp. 143-68, for examples.

There are several tests available for determining whether residuals are normally distributed (see Maddala, 1977, pp. 305-6). For simulation studies examining small sample properties of commonly used tests, the reader is referred to Shapiro, Wilk and Chen (1968) and Huang and Block (1974). When working with a single cross-section or a single time series, Box and Cox (1964) have examined analytically a family of transformations to correct for asymmetry in the residual distributions. Maximum likelihood estimates of the transforming parameters are obtained with a method that is particularly simple to implement. This technique can be extended to models of pooled cross-sectional and time series data provided that maximum likelihood estimation is used and that the likelihood using these estimates can be computed (see Chang and Lee, 1977 for an example involving the error components model).

FIGURE 5.9
TESTING ASSUMPTIONS ABOUT RESIDUALS

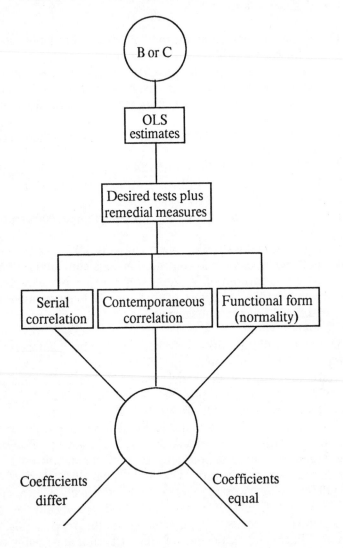

The Box and Cox procedure was extended for this research to the RCR and mixed RCR models. Some preliminary results are reported in an article by Dielman, et al. (1978).[3] These tests should enter the analysis at points B and C of Figure 5.8. It is at this point when initial (OLS) estimation of models takes place. Before trying to determine whether coefficients differ from one cross-section to another we follow Maddala's suggestion and run an OLS regression for each individual unit and examine the residuals. This examination may consist of classical procedures or tests performed using the procedures developed in Chapter 4.

In Figure 5.9 we append the Figure 5.8 flowchart to demonstrate when tests of residual assumptions and appropriate remedial measures should take place.

Section 5.3 Variable Choice

The problem of variable selection in linear regression models is one of considerable depth. Section 5.3 is not intended to provide full coverage in this area. A survey of the variable selection problem and some suggestions for determining the "best" subset of variables can be found in Hocking (1976). The material to be presented in this section applies to the RCR and mixed RCR models.

The importance of deciding which variables to include and which to delete from a regression model is emphasized by a consideration of forecasting. We examine here certain results concerning the precision of forecasts in the case of a single time series regression equation. The effect of these results on variable selection in the RCR model and the implications for hypothesis testing procedures will be examined. Finally, the hypothesis testing procedures used to select variables in the RCR and mixed RCR models will be reviewed along with some considerations for their use based on previously presented results.

Suppose our model is written

$$\underline{Y}_i = X_i \underline{b}_i + \underline{e}_i \qquad i = 1, \ldots, N, \qquad (5.6)$$

where

$\underline{b}_i$ is a $K \times 1$ vector of coefficients,
X_i is a $T \times K$ matrix of observations on the independent variables,
$\underline{Y}_i$ is a $T \times 1$ vector of observations on the dependent variable, and
$\underline{e}_i$ is a $T \times 1$ vector of random disturbances.

Suppose we want to predict a single drawing of the dependent variable for a cross-sectional unit, i, which is one of the original N units of our sample. We will denote the vector of regressors for the prediction period by X_i^*. Swamy (1971, pp. 133-34) has shown that the minimum variance linear unbiased (MVLU) predictor for y_i is given by

$$\hat{y}_i^* = X_i^{*\prime} \hat{\underline{b}}_i \qquad (5.7)$$

where

$\hat{\underline{b}}_i$ is the OLS estimate of $\underline{b}_i$.

The variance of the forecast error is

$$E(\hat{y}_i^* - y_i^*)^2 = \sigma_i^2 (1 + \underline{X}_i^{*\prime} (X_i^{\prime} X_i)^{-1} \underline{X}_i^*) \qquad (5.8)$$

where

y_i^* is the true value of y_i in the prediction period, and $\sigma_i^2 = E(\underline{e}_i^{\prime} \underline{e}_i)$.

The result in equation (5.7) means that MVLU forecasts of the independent variable for an individual unit in the RCR model are obtained in the same manner as MVLU forecasts of this one unit when it is viewed as a separate equation apart from the others and estimated by OLS. This result can be combined with results presented by Hocking (1976) to provide some insight into why proper variable selection techniques are necessary.

Suppose equation (5.6) has been written

$$\underline{Y}_i = X_{ip} \underline{b}_{ip} + X_{ir} \underline{b}_{ir} + \underline{e}_i. \qquad (5.9)$$

Here we have partitioned X_i and $\underline{b}_i$ according to certain variables (those subscripted by r) which we are considering for deletion from our model. Hocking provides us with several results which indicate the importance such deletions may hold for the precision of our forecasts. These results are summarized as follows:

The forecast error variance is never smaller using the model with X_{ir} and X_{ip} included than when we use the model with the X_{ir} deleted. Thus, even if $\underline{b}_{ir} \neq 0$, future responses may be predicted with smaller variance using the model with the X_{ir} omitted. In this case the penalty is in the bias which will be present in the forecast. Hocking also provides conditions under which the gain in precision is not offset by the bias. Thus, in a separate equation regression, we can formulate conditions under which variable deletion is appropriate.[4]

When should variables be deleted from the RCR (or mixed RCR) models? This question is more complex when asked in the RCR context than when asked in the context of separate equation regressions. In the latter we can use t- or F-tests to determine whether coefficients are significantly different from zero. If they are not, we omit the associated variable from the model. This procedure is also acceptable in the mixed RCR context when examining fixed coefficients. Random coefficients present more of a problem, however. We have procedures available to test whether the mean of a random coefficient(s) is different from zero. If we find we must accept an hypothesis of zero mean for a particular random coefficient we cannot automatically delete the associated variable from the model. Variation in a coefficient may be as important a reason for allowing a variable to remain in a model as is having a non-zero mean. Even though a coefficient may have zero mean, the coefficient itself may be significantly different from zero for certain individual units from our sample. Thus the variation in the coefficient may indicate that the variable is important for some cross-sectional units and not for others.

Relating this to Hocking's forecasting results we can see that deletion of the variable will not produce a bias in the forecast for certain of the individuals in our sample but it may do so for others. We have no way of knowing whether the total bias for our N sample firms is small enough to warrant deletion of the variable corresponding to the random coefficient with mean zero. Thus deletion of such a variable involves a tradeoff between bias and precision of forecast that has not yet been fully investigated.

Proper specification of the behavior of coefficients in our models thus appears to be of considerable importance. To aid in this specification we have several hypothesis testing procedures available. Hypothesis testing procedures for coefficients in an RCR or mixed RCR model were developed by Zellner and Swamy (see Appendix C) and were extended in Chapter 3. The tests which are now available are outlined below.[5]

1. A Test for Randomness of the Full Vector or Partitions of the Full Vector of Random Coefficients.

The statistic for testing randomness of the full coefficient vector is given in equation (C.29) of Appendix C. Under the null hypothesis that coefficient vectors are equal over all cross-sectional units, the statistic has a chi-square distribution with $K_1(N-1)$ degrees of freedom where K_1 is the number of coefficients (the number of components of the vector) and N is the number of cross-sectional units in the sample.

A test for randomness of only a subset of the coefficients in our model is suggested in Chapter 3. The statistic used to perform this test, labelled C, is shown in equation (3.41). Under the null hypothesis that the partitions of the coefficient vector are equal for all cross-sectional units, C has a χ^2-distribution with $H_1 \cdot (N\text{-}1)$ degrees of freedom. Here H_1 is the number of components of the partition (the number of coefficients to be tested for randomness) and N is the number of cross-sectional units in the sample.

2. A Test for Mean Equal Zero for the
Full Vector or Partitions of the Coefficient Vector
(This test can be applied to both fixed and random coefficients.)

Swamy developed a test to determine whether the vector of coefficient means, $\bar{b}$, is equal to zero.[6] The test statistic is shown in equation (C.24) of Appendix C. Under the null hypothesis that $\bar{b} = 0$, the statistic is distributed as F with K_1 and $N\text{-}K_1$ degrees of freedom. Here, K_1 is the number of coefficients included in the test for mean zero and N is the sample size.

In Chapter 3, equation (3.13) shows the test statistic for partitions of the vector of coefficient means. Under the null hypothesis that the means included in the partition are equal to zero, the statistic has the F-distribution with H_1 and $N\text{-}H_1$ degrees of freedom. H_1 is the number of coefficient means to be tested and N is the sample size.

The tests for mean zero can also be used on partitions which include fixed coefficients. In this case we are simply testing whether the coefficient value is zero. For computational purposes the test procedure is exactly as before except that the variances of the coefficients assumed to be fixed are constrained to equal zero.

A special case of this test was examined in some detail in Section 3.2 of Chapter 3. This special case is the use of the t-statistic for testing whether a single coefficient mean or a fixed coefficient is equal to zero. The examination considers instances when negative variance estimates are obtained for certain coefficients using RCR estimation. This result often leads us to revise our assumptions about the randomness of these coefficients and view them as fixed. We then re-estimate the model with the variances of these coefficients constrained to equal zero. The value of t-statistics calculated under the fixed assumption will often differ drastically from the value under the assumption of randomness. Our analysis shows that this is to be expected. Thus, inferences from the model where negative variance estimates are obtained can be misleading. The researcher is, therefore, cautioned against using inferences based on t-statistics (and the more general F-statistic) calculated when negative variance estimates are obtained.

3. A Simultaneous Test of Randomness and Mean Equal Zero.

This test is developed in Chapter 3 and the test statistic, S, is given in equation (3.43). As shown, it can be applied to the full vector of random coefficients or to partitions of the vector of random coefficients. Under the null hypothesis that the H_1 coefficients included in the test are fixed and equal to zero, S has a chi-square distribution with $N \cdot H_1$ degrees of freedom. As in the previous tests, N is the number of cross-sectional units in the sample.

As a final note in the use of these tests, we reconsider the comments made concerning negative variance estimates and their effects on inferences using random coefficient techniques. As mentioned under Test (2) it is possible that test statistics from an RCR model with negative variance estimates can provide misleading or obviously incorrect conclusions. For this reason we suggest the following approach be used with the RCR model when using any of the tests in a model specification process:

(1) Estimate the model with all coefficients assumed random.
(2) If negative variance estimates occur, constrain the variances of the respective coefficients to equal zero.
(3) Re-estimate the model as a mixed RCR model (or a classical pooled regression if all variances have been constrained to equal zero). At this stage the tests described above may be used appropriately. Models can then be respecified on the basis of inferences from the tests.

By following the above procedure we eliminate the possibility that a negative variance estimate might somehow bias our test results.

Section 5.4 Summary

Chapter 5 presents a schema for the analysis of pooled cross-sectional and time series data. The intention of the schema is to provide the empirical researcher with guidelines for:

(1) Deciding which model is appropriate for his data;
(2) Testing assumptions made about residuals; and
(3) Selecting variables to be included in the model.

In Chapter 6 we apply the schema and certain results of previous chapters in an analysis of stock market data.

Chapter 6

Analysis of the Effects of Repurchasing Stock

Section 6.1 Historical Perspective

The application of a firm's resources to the repurchase of its own stock has become increasingly popular in recent years. Guthart (1965) first compiled data on repurchasing activity. Stewart (1976) extended this compilation through 1974. The results of their research are combined in Table 6.1 for the years 1957 to 1974.

As firms became more active in this process of reacquisition of common stock, interest developed in the economics of share repurchasing and the implications it might have concerning share valuation. Bierman and West (1966) first used a valuation model to study corporate stock repurchasing. The major result of their research was to place emphasis on the tax advantage to be gained from repurchasing shares as opposed to the payment of dividends. They suggest that this advantage is the most important factor in fostering the increase in repurchasing. Elton and Gruber (1968) responded to this suggestion by presenting a valuation model of their own which, they claimed, was more realistic than the model of Bierman and West. They suggest that any tax advantage associated with repurchasing may be "more than offset" by increases in transaction costs for stockholders in certain firms.

Other than a tax advantage, there are several possible motivations for a firm to repurchase shares of its own common stock. Some firms are thought to repurchase their own shares due to a lack of better investments. The actual motivation here can be traced back to the tax effect. The firm intends to increase stockholders' wealth by distributing excess funds. A repurchase is chosen over a dividend due to the differential tax rates on dividends and capital gains. Firms may also repurchase from stockholders who own small numbers of shares in order to control stockholder servicing costs. A discussion of these and other motives and a review of the literture can be found in Marks (1976) and in Dann (1978).

Table 6.1
Repurchasing Activity of NYSE Firms

Year	Gross Shares Repurchased During Year
1957	8,379,798
1958	9,818,530
1959	11,883,792
1960	12,791,260
1961	14,928,674
1962	23,310,548
1963	29,277,781
1964	44,031,442
1965	45,155,977
1966	46,112,064
1967	27,272,127
1968	44,006,311
1969	63,492,471
1970	50,633,213
1971	40,748,500
1972	43,883,724
1973	143,780,086
1974	90,379,654

Concurrent with the theoretical work of Bierman and West, and Elton and Gruber, we find a major empirical investigation of the motivations for repurchasing stock and of the impact of repurchasing on stock price. This study by Young (1967) suggests that the performance of firms subsequent to repurchase is, at best, equivalent to that of the market in a statistically significant number of cases.[1] In other words, Young found no significant short run price effects. Following Young, there seems to have been a five year pause in the study of repurchasing. However, by 1973 repurchasing activity had increased in intensity, and the interest in studying this phenomenon was rekindled.

Section 6.2 Recent Findings

Recent literature can be classified by its concern with two issues: 1) what are the operating and financial characteristics of firms that repurchase their own stock; and 2) what effect does the repurchase have on the price of the stock and on the wealth of the stockholders.

On the first issue, the consensus is that firms repurchasing their own stock have less leverage, inferior operating performance, and they experience slower growth than is the case for non-repurchasing firms. Agreement on these results is widespread. Support is found in the research of Norgaard and Norgaard (1974) and Rosenberg and Young (1978).

On the second issue the current research provides ambiguous answers. To aid in our review of this research we first classify repurchases according to the two most common methods: tender offer and open market repurchase. With a tender offer, the company makes a formal offer to its stockholdres to purchase shares of its stock. With open market repurchases, a company buys its stock through a brokerage house. Therefore, in an open market repurchase, there may have been no announcement to stockholders of the intention to repurchase.[2] Also, open market repurchases are often very small in comparison to tender offer repurchases. As a result of the differences in these two types of repurchases their effects on the price of stock may differ. Thus, open market and tender offer repurchases are often analyzed separately.

In this review we will indicate whether a separate or combined analysis has been performed.

Stewart (1976) combined both tender offer and open market firms and found that the effect of repurchasing on stock price is neutral in the short run. However, he found positive long run effects requiring more than two years to show up in price performance. This result implies a rather inefficient market and may be inconsistent with empirical evidence on market efficiency.[3] Rosenberg and Young (1976), using a sample of tender offer repurchases, examined the price performance of their firms relative to the market as a whole. In general, they found the tendered securities outperformed the market (as measured by the Standard & Poor's 500 composite index) only in periods just before the repurchase announcement. Nantell and Finnerty (1978), using a sample of large tender offers and adjusting for the dilution effects of the premium paid in repurchasing shares, found an immediate and significant positive effect on stockholder wealth. A previous analysis by Nantell and Finnerty (1974) obtained similar results for a sample of tender offer firms and, in addition, they found neutral effects for an open market sample. Marks (1976) also studied open market and tender offer repurchases separately. He found that, for open market repurchases, there was no price effect. For tender offers, he found an immediate positive price effect in agreement with the Nantell and Finnerty studies. Marks, however, found this positive effect to be somewhat offset when the tender offer terminated. He attributes this result to a dilution in per share value due to repurchasing at a premium. Recall that Nantell and Finnerty (1978) perform their analysis after adjusting for this effect using a valuation model developed explicitly for this purpose. They find no evidence that the positive effect is offset for their sample.

Dann (1978), in an unpublished paper, used daily data to investigate announcement effects for a sample of tender offers. He found positive effects beginning a few days before the announcement with a cumulative increase of nearly 25% as of the announcement date.

On the question of price effects then, we see no clearcut consensus as we did on the question of firm characteristics. Consulting the theory of stock repurchasing we can gain some insights into why this is to be expected. These insights pertain to possible motivations for a repurchase of stock. We can attach either a positive or negative connotation to each of these motivations depending on the pricing implications they are felt to have for a firm's stock.

On the positive side is the argument that if the repurchase of stock is a replacement for a cash dividend, then tax advantages are generated by the repurchase. This is the argument of Bierman and West (1966) previously discussed. Another positive argument is that the repurchase is indicative of management's view that the stock is undervalued and is therefore a profitable investment. Such a statement by management could cause the market to revalue the security. Research by Jaffe (1974) and Finnerty (1976) provides evidence of management's ability to identify when its own stock is undervalued. Finally, Young and Marshall (1967) have pointed out the advantages of repurchasing as a means of controlling stockholder servicing costs.

On the negative side, the classical position is that announcing a stock repurchase is announcing to the market that your firm has "run out of" profitable investment opportunities. This argument implies a negative relationship between repurchasing and prices only to the extent that the announcement represents a new piece of information for the market.

Since repurchasing may affect the firm's capital structure we may have a price shift due to this change also. The argument as to whether this effect is positive or negative is quite complicated, however, and the determination of the direction of this effect is unclear. In this instance we also face the ambiguous state of capital structure theory (see Haugen and Senbet, 1978).[4]

In conclusion, we find that the theoretical price and wealth effects of a stock repurchase are not clear. The motivations involved in each repurchase may give rise to either positive, neutral, or negative effects. This fact can help us to understand why conflicting results were obtained in the empirical studies discussed previously. These studies all assume that they are dealing with a homogeneous sample of repurchasing firms in drawing their conclusions. It is likely, however, that motivations for repurchasing will differ for different firms in any sample. To draw conclusions from the statistics derived from using a heterogeneous sample ignores the problem that significant price effects for different firms with different motivations may simply be offsetting one another. In such a situation, we might conclude that the price effects of a repurchase are neutral, when in fact they are positive for some firms in the sample and negative for others. Thus, a methodology is needed that allows us to investigate whether the price effects of a repurchase are fixed or whether they vary from firm to firm, and, in either case, to determine the magnitude and sign of the individual and the overall effects.

Section 6.3 Suggestions for Further Analysis

Many of the recent studies of repurchasing activity have used residual analysis as the major technique for determining overall price effects from the repurchase announcement. As noted in Appendix A there are drawbacks to the use of this approach. In view of these drawbacks we suggested an alternative approach designed to analyze the effect of a release of information about the firm on the rate of return. In Chapter 2 we combined this alternative approach with econometric techniques for analyzing pooled cross-sectional and time series data in order to achieve a further improvement. These econometric models were designed to more effectively utilize our data in the calculation of certain statistics. They provide us with a theoretical basis for using these statistics to make inferences about population parameters of interest. In Chapter 5 we suggested a schema designed to aid the researcher in his choice of model specification. An appropriate model specification includes proper assumptions concerning

1) the coefficients in our linear model
2) the disturbances in our model
3) the variables to be included in the model

In this chapter we demonstrate the use of the schema in an analysis of the effects of firms' announcements that they plan to repurchase their own stock. Through the model specification process described in Chapter 5 we hope to arrive at a methodology which will correct some of the shortcomings of previous analyses.

Section 6.4 The Market Model

Most of the recent empirical results concerning repurchase announcement effects are risk-adjusted results. The basic risk-adjustment procedure relates in one way or another to residual analysis,[5] and to the use of the market model described in Chapter 2:

$$R_{it} = a_i + b_i R_{mt} + e_{it} \qquad\qquad (6.1)$$

where

R_{it} = rate of return on security i in time period t;
R_{mt} = rate of return on the market in time period t;[6]
a_i and b_i are unknown parameters;
e_{it} is a random disturbance term.

This form of the market model is due to Sharpe (1963) and allows us to make adjustments for general market conditions represented by the term R_{mt}.

An alternative formulation of the model in (6.1) is suggested by Black, Jensen and Scholes (1973):

$$R_{it}^* = a_i + b_i R_{mt}^* + e_{it} \qquad\qquad (6.2)$$

where

$R_{it}^* = R_{it} - R_{ft}$;
$R_{mt}^* = R_{mt} - R_{ft}$;
R_{ft} = risk-free rate of return; in this case the risk-free rates are monthly rates on three-month treasury bills. The other terms are as previously defined.

By introducing the risk free rate, the model is actually being fit to excess returns above the risk-free rate on the securities and on the market. It is an amended form of the model in (6.2) which will be used throughout our analysis.[7]

Section 6.5 Data

The period from 1957 through 1974 was scanned to find firms that repurchased their stock either by way of open market repurchases or through tender offers. Annual reports and 10-K reports served as the main sources for identifying possible repurchases for our sample. Given this list of repurchases, the *Wall Street Journal* was searched to identify the date of the repurchase announcement. From the original list, we found announcement dates for 174 repurchases by 139 firms.[8] Of these 77 were repurchases by way of tender offers from 70 firms, and 97 were accomplished by open market action by 77 firms. Note that some firms repurchased two or three times during the period in question. Also, there were instances of firms with multiple repurchases where both methods of repurchases were used. Of the 25 firms which repurchased twice, 4 repurchased once by tender offer and once by open market action. Of the five firms repurchasing exactly three times, only one used the same method for all three repurchases. The information above is summarized in Table 6.2.

Monthly rates of return for the securities in the sample were obtained from the CRSP tapes.[9] Returns for 107 months preceding the first repurchase announcement and 60 months following the last recorded announcement were included. The return on the market was also taken from the CRSP data set.

Table 6.2
Description of the Sample of Repurchasing Firms

	Tender Offer	Open Market
Number of firms	70	77
Total number of repurchases	77	97

a. Repurchase Method

	Number of Firms
Exactly one repurchase	109
Exactly two repurchases	25
Exactly three repurchases	5

b. Number of Repurchases

As a risk-free rate we used monthly rates on three-month treasury bills. These rates are compiled by the Federal Reserve,[10] and were obtained from the NBER database.

Section 6.6 Hypotheses

Several questions concerning the effects of repurchase announcement on share price were suggested in the review of the literature. These questions will form the basic hypotheses to be tested in our study. The first question involves the behavior of the rate of return in time periods preceding the announcement. If there is any preannouncement leakage of information about the forthcoming repurchase we might expect return to change in time periods preceding the announcement. These changes reflect the leakage of information concerning the firm to the market.

The next question involves the month of announcement itself. If the announcement carries any new information with it regarding the value of the security, this should be reflected in the return for that security. And if the market is fairly efficient, as seems to be the case, the impact of the new information should be reflected very quickly. Thus we may encounter a change in the rate of return for a firm's stock in the month of announcement if the market views this event as containing new information about the firm.

Finally, there are questions concerning what happens to the return after announcement. Even if the market reacts favorably to the information contained in the announcement and the return rises in the month of announcement, this may be due to the premium paid on repurchase. In this case we would find offsetting behavior in subsequent months and price may fall back to its previous level. These are the pricing effects that will be investigated.

A further question that has recently begun to draw interest concerns the effect that a repurchase announement might have on the systematic risk of stocks. Marks (1976) investigated the question using the market model in (6.1) to obtain estimates of b_i, the beta coefficient, both before and after repurchase. He then averaged the beta's for all the firms in his sample and found that:

1) The average beta increased significantly after repurchase for firms with open market repurchases (number of firms = 138).
2) The average beta increased from before to after repurchase for tender offer firms but the increase was not statistically significant (number of firms = 42).

The question of a change in systematic risk after repurchase announcement will be further examined in this study using an alternative methodology.

Section 6.7 Model Specification and Hypothesis Tests

The concept of significance of variables in a random coefficient model, as mentioned in Chapter 5, is more difficult to define than in a fixed coefficient regression model. For example, in our final models we want to include non-zero fixed coefficients and all random coefficients, whether or not their means are zero. We feel that randomness of a coefficient adds to the explanatory power of the model even if the mean of that coefficient is zero. Thus, variables are omitted from the model only if hypothesis testing procedures show that their coefficients are both fixed and equal to zero.

We review here the three different types of hypothesis tests found especially useful. The first of these generalizes the t-test for the significance of an individual variable in an ordinary regression model. In the case of random coefficients, we are concerned with the population mean (across firms) of the coefficient of an individual variable, and we test the hypothesis that this mean is equal to zero. Our models also may include variables with coefficients assumed to be fixed and identical across firms, and in this case our hypothesis is that the coefficient itself is equal to zero. For simplicity of exposition we will refer to the mean of the coefficient regardless of whether the coefficient is random or fixed. In either case our hypothesis is tested with a generalized t-statistic using an asymptotic t-distribution with N-1 degrees of freedom, where N is the number of firms in the sample.[11]

Our second procedure is a test of the hypothesis that the coefficients of a specific subset of the variables simultaneouly all have mean equal to zero. As already noted, if some of the specified variables have coefficients assumed to be fixed, our hypothesis is equivalent to stating that these coefficients are equal to zero. The hypothesis is tested with a generalized F-statistic using an asymptotic F-distribution with L and N-L degrees of freedom, where L is the number of coefficients included in the test.[12]

Finally, we can test for the randomness of one coefficient or several coefficients simultaneously. We use a test statistic having a Chi-square distribution under the null hypothesis that the coefficients are fixed and identical across firms. The statistic has L·N degrees of freedom.[13]

Section 6.8 Demonstration of Schema

Suppose we are interested in an analysis of repurchasing firms using the market model in (6.2). We want to estimate the average "beta" coefficient for these securities; i.e., our interest lies in an overall estimate rather than firm-by-firm estimates. We will use the schema presented in Chapter 5 to structure such an analysis. Results from this initial examination of the market model will be used to facilitate the investigation of repurchase effects.

Since we desire overall estimates we have passed the first decision point of the schema (see Figure 5.1). We must now ask whether the coefficients of the market model are the same for all firms or whether they differ (see Figure 5.4). We can use either the Zellner technique (described in Appendix C and in Chapter 3, equation (3.38) and (3.40)) or the classical F-test described in Chapter 5. We will choose the Zellner test for two reasons:

(1) The time series length, T, is large, so the Zellner test is justified;
(2) The variances of the separate regressions (the unsystematic risks) are known to differ from stock to stock. Zellner's test takes explicit account of this fact.

The value of the test statistic for testing the hypothesis

$$H_o: a_1 = a_2 \ldots = a_n = a \qquad\qquad (6.3)$$

$$\text{and } b_1 = b_2 = \ldots = b_n = b$$

is 1257.85

The statistic has a Chi-square distribution with $(N-1) \cdot K = 276$ degrees of freedom. For 276 degrees of freedom the critical value corresponding to a 1% significance level is 333.7.[14] Thus, we reject the hypothesis in (6.3) and conclude that one or both of the coefficients in the model differ from firm to firm.

At this point in the schema we can test residuals from the OLS regressions for any systematic pattern as suggested by Maddala. For example, we can use the pooled test for serial correlation developed in Chapter 4 to test whether the serial correlation coefficients for all of our 139 firms are equal to zero. Results of this test are summarized in Table 6.3. At the 1% level of significance we must reject the hypothesis that all correlation coefficients are zero. After generalized differencing of the data, the pooled test results in Table 6.4 show that any possible first order serial correlation has been removed. The hypothesis that all serial correlation coefficients are equal to zero is accepted at the 1% level of significance.[15]

We are now at decision point J in the schema (see Figure 5.6). We must decide whether to estimate the coefficients as fixed and different or as random. The option for random coefficients is chosen here for several reasons:

(1) Coefficients differ from firm to firm.
(2) We are interested in overall market effects rather than individual firm effects. The RCR model will allow us a better theoretical base for inference to the population of firms than, say, the separate regression approach described in Appendix A.
(3) We can perform analyses using the RCR model that would not be possible with the separate equation methodology (e.g., simultaneous inference and certain analyses of the beta coefficients).

The RCR estimates of the model are shown in Table 6.5. Note that the population variance of the constant term, a, has a negative estimate. Following the suggestions in the schema we constrained this variance to be zero, thus treating the constant term as fixed (see decision point L of Figure 5.7). The results in the table indicate an average beta for our repurchasing firms of 1.03 and a fixed value of the constant term of .003. We also note that there is significant variation in the betas as indicated by our estimate of the population standard deviation, .329.

In Table 6.6 results of RCR estimation are shown for the model after generalized differencing to remove serial correlation. As can be seen, the estimates and standard errors are nearly the same as those from the model before differencing. In general we found this to be the case for all subsequent models to be presented. Thus we have chosen in those cases to neglect the differencing process since the final results seem to be the same.

To facilitate further the examination of additional models to be presented throughout this chapter we will begin our discussion at point L in the schema (see Figure 5.7). As with the market model, when the Zellner test is applied to each of the subsequent models we find that we must reject the hypothesis that all coefficients are equal across all firms. We have, for reasons previously stated, chosen the random coefficient model to analyze our data. At point L in the schema we are therefore faced with two questions in regard to proper model specification:

(1) Are all coefficients random or are certain of the coefficients in our model fixed?
(2) Which variables should be included in a properly specified model?

The answers to these questions will provide us with information concerning the effect of repurchase announcement on both rate of return and systematic risk.

TABLE 6.3

POOLED TEST FOR SERIAL CORRELATION
FOR THE MARKET MODEL

Pooled estimate of the serial correlation coefficient	Test of $H_0 : p=0,$ t	Simultaneous test of $H_0 : p_1 = p_2 = \ldots = p_N = p = 0,$ χ^2
-0.102	-15.0	442.8
1% critical value [16]	2.6	179.6
Degrees of freedom	138	138

TABLE 6.4

POOLED TEST FOR SERIAL CORRELATION
AFTER DIFFERENCING

Pooled estimate of the serial correlation coefficient	Test of $H_0 : p=0,$ t	Simultaneous test of $H_0 : p_1 = p_2 = \ldots = p_N = p = 0,$ χ^2
-0.005	-0.7	4.9
1% critical value	2.6	179.6
Degrees of freedom	138	138

TABLE 6.5
RCR ESTIMATES FOR THE MARKET MODEL

Coefficient	Mean	Population standard deviation	Test for mean zero, t	Test for randomness, χ^2
a	0.003	*	7.0	
b_i	1.030	0.329	34.5	1097.0
1% critical value			2.6	179.6
Degrees of freedom			138	138

TABLE 6.6
RCR ESTIMATES FOR THE MARKET MODEL
AFTER CORRECTING FOR SERIAL CORRELATION

Coefficient	Mean	Population standard deviation	Test for mean zero, t	Test for randomness, χ^2
a	0.003	*	7.6	
b_i	1.034	0.331	34.6	1193.3
1% critical value			2.6	179.6
Degrees of freedom			138	138

* Coefficients constrained to be fixed (i.e., those with zero variance restrictions imposed) are indicated by an asterisk (*).

Section 6.9 Effects of Repurchase Announcement on Rate of Return

The basic model we would like to estimate in order to determine the effects of repurchase announcement on rate of return can be written as:[17]

$$R_{it}{}^* = a_i + b_i R_{mt}{}^* + C_{o;i} Z_{o;it} \\ + C_{-1;i} Z_{-1;it} + C_{-2;i} Z_{-2;it} + C_{-3;i} Z_{-3;it} \\ + C_{+1;i} Z_{+1;it} + \ldots + C_{+6;i} Z_{+6;it} + e_{it} \tag{6.4}$$

where

$R_{it}{}^*$ and $R_{mt}{}^*$ are as previously defined;

$$Z_{0;it} = \begin{cases} 1 \text{ if firm i announced a repurchase} \\ \quad \text{ in time period t} \\ 0 \text{ otherwise} \end{cases}$$

$$Z_{+k;it} = \begin{cases} 1 \text{ in the } k^{th} \text{ time period following any} \\ \quad \text{ announcement made by firm i} \\ 0 \text{ otherwise} \end{cases}$$

$$Z_{-k;it} = \begin{cases} 1 \text{ in the } k^{th} \text{ time period preceding any} \\ \quad \text{ announcement made by firm i} \\ 0 \text{ otherwise} \end{cases}$$

In this model, the coefficient $C_{o;i}$ of $Z_{o;it}$ measures any excess return in the month of announcement, i.e., any immediate effect. Since premiums above market prices are paid when repurchasing through tender offers, Marks (1976) and others have argued that to capture the entire price effects of a repurchase, returns must be analyzed through the repurchase period. One possiblility is that $C_{o;i}$ is positive due only to the premium paid, and that once this premium is removed, prices retreat. To account for this possibility, we added dummy variables to check on returns subsequent to the announcement. For instance, the explanatory variable $Z_{+1;it}$ is a dummy variable indicating the first month subsequent to announcement. If its coefficient, $C_{+1;i}$, equals zero then we would conclude that any excess return during the announcement month was not canceled during the month following the announcement. In addition, a series of three dummy variables, $Z_{-1;it}$, $Z_{-2;it}$, and $Z_{-3;it}$ were included to test whether there were any information leakages prior to the announcement.

The tests were run separately on the open market sample and on the tender offer sample. The results are presented in Tables 6.7 and 6.8, respectively.

Section 6.10 Open Market Sample

For the open market sample, the announcement effect and subsequent month effects are examined in Panel A of Table 6.7. Recall that coefficients with negative variance estimates on initial estimation are constrained to be fixed. Fixed coefficients are denoted by an asterisk in the Population Standard Deviation column. Panel A shows that the coefficients for the first, second, and third months after announcement are both fixed and not significantly different from zero. The subsequent month coefficients for the fourth, fifth, and sixth months are significantly random but have mean zero. These conclusions follow from the simultaneous tests reported in the final column. No specific conclusions regarding the effects of repurchasing should be drawn until the model is re-estimated leaving out those variables with fixed coefficients equal to zero.

In Panel B of Table 6.7 we have deleted those subsequent month indicators whose coefficients were both fixed and equal to zero. We also have added the prior month indicators. None of the prior coefficients appear to be random. The simultaneous F-test results also show their means to be zero.

When tested for randomness the month of announcement coefficient also appears to be fixed. From the small t-statistic value we conclude that no significant change in rate of return occurs during the announcement month.

Panel C presents our final model containing all coefficients exhibiting randomness and/or a mean value different from zero. We found no significant month of announcement effect and no effect due to leakage of information prior to the announcement. Subsequent effects are insignificant for the first three month following repurchase. In the fourth, fifth and sixth subsequent months there is unexpected variability in the behavior of security return, but on the average these subsequent effects are not significantly different from zero. This final result again follows from the simultaneous test for mean equal zero applied to the three remaining subsequent month coefficients. Our conclusion is that there were uniformly no price effects for the sample of firms repurchasing by way of open market operations.

In Figure 6.1 we have plotted the means of the coefficients as given by their final values in Table 6.7. This graphical presentation of the coefficient means further supports the conclusion that, on the average, there are no price effects for the open market sample.[18]

Table 6.7
RCR Estimates for Open Market Sample

Coefficient	Mean	Population Standard Deviation*	Test for mean Zero, t	Simultaneous Test Results Randomness, χ^2	Test Mean Zero, F

A. Subsequent Month and Month of Announcement Indicators

Coefficient	Mean	Pop. Std. Dev.*	Test mean Zero, t	Randomness, χ^2	Mean Zero, F
a_i	0.003	*	4.9		
b_i	0.988	0.373	21.6		
$C_{o;i}$	0.027	0.045	3.0		
$C_{+1;i}$	-0.003	*	-0.4		
$C_{+2;i}$	0.003	*	0.5		
$C_{+3;i}$	-0.003	*	-0.4		
$C_{+4;i}$	0.005	0.045	0.6		} -2.0
$C_{+5;i}$	0.028	0.064	2.7	} 311.6	
$C_{+6;i}$	-0.002	0.034	-0.2		
1% critical value			2.6	277.4	3.1
Degrees of freedom**			72	225	6,67

B. Prior Month Indicators Added

Coefficient	Mean	Pop. Std. Dev.*	Test mean Zero, t	Randomness, χ^2	Mean Zero, F
a_i	0.003	*	5.0		
b_i	0.999	0.368	21.7		
$C_{o;i}$	0.010	0.047	1.1	99.0	
$C_{+4;i}$	-0.004	0.042	-0.4		
$C_{+5;i}$	0.020	0.064	1.8	} 311.1	} 1.4
$C_{+6;i}$	-0.010	0.034	-1.1		
$C_{-1;i}$	-0.006	0.030	-0.8	105.3	
$C_{-2;i}$	-0.009	*	-1.2		} .7
$C_{-3;i}$	0.001	*	0.1		
1% critical value			2.6	277.4 106.5	4.1
Degrees of freedom			69	225 75	3,67

C. Final Model

Coefficient	Mean	Pop. Std. Dev.*	Test mean Zero, t	Randomness, χ^2	Mean Zero, F
a_i	0.003	*	5.0		
b_i	0.974	0.366	22.2		
$C_{+4;i}$	0.003	0.044	0.4		
$C_{+5;i}$	0.025	0.064	2.4	} 307.9	} 2.8
$C_{+6;i}$	-0.003	0.033	-0.3		
1% critical value			2.6	277.4	4.1
Degrees of freedom			75	255	3,73

Section 6.11 Tender Offer Sample

The findings given in Table 6.8 for the tender offer sample differ considerably from those for the open market sample. The most important change in findings is that the coefficient $C_{o;i}$, the announcement effect on security return, is random and it is on the average signficantly positive. For open market repurchases, we could not reject the hypothesis that this coefficient was fixed and equal to zero.

In Panel A of Table 6.8 we investigate the behavior of security returns for the six months following the month of announcement. The simultaneous test for randomness applied to the coefficients $C_{+1;i}$, $C_{+2;i}$, $C_{+5;i}$, and $C_{+6;i}$, yields a value for the test statistic that is not significant at the 1% level. The simultaneous test for mean zero applied to all six subsequent month indicators yields a value for the F-statistic of .8. This, too, is not significant at the 1% level. Thus the coefficient $C_{+1;i}$, . . ., $C_{+6;i}$ can be viewed appropriately as being fixed and equal to zero, thus adding no explanatory power to the model. Again it appears that there is no significant price roll back after the premium tender offer is removed.

In Panel B the three months prior to announcement are investigated to see if any leakage of information might have occurred. Initial estimation resulted in negative variances for these three coefficients. The true variances are thus constrained to equal zero. The F-test indicates that these three coefficients are also equal to zero and may be omitted from the final model shown in Panel C.

The only month when any significant effect is found for the tender offer sample is the month of the announcement. Thus, in our final model we omit the prior and subsequent month indicators. As shown in Panel C, the announcement effect does vary from stock to stock (population standard deviation = 0.130). The average effect is positive and significantly different from zero. On average we see that security return increases by 9.7% in the month of announcement. Apparently, the tax advantages of the repurchase along with undervaluation signalling, and improved captial structure generally dominate any inference that the firms have "run out of" investment opportunities. However, the randomness of the $C_{o;i}$ coefficient emphasizes that our tender offer

---

*Coefficients constrained to be fixed (i.e., those with zero variance restrictions imposed) are indicated by an asterisk (*).

**A small number of firms had to be discarded from the estimates, t-tests, and F-tests because of matrix inversion difficulties. Three firms were affected in Panel A, six in Panel B, and none in Panel C. However, all 76 firms were used to calculate the χ^2 statistic.

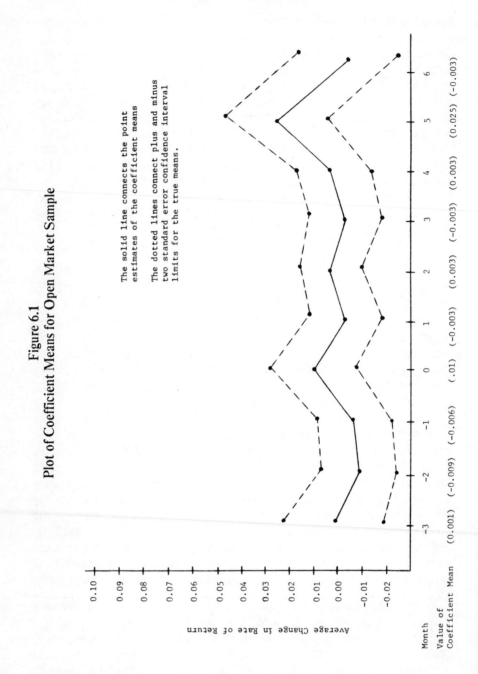

Figure 6.1
Plot of Coefficient Means for Open Market Sample

sample is not homogeneous with respect to price effects, and is probably not homogeneous with respect to the motivation for repurchasing. Hence, we could not universally recommend stock repurchasing even though the average price effects are positive.

Figure 6.2 is a plot of coefficient means from the models in Table 6.8. Our conclusions are again supported. The increase in the average rate of return for securities of tender offer firms is much greater during the month of announcement than in any of the prior or subsequent months.[18]

Section 6.12 Changes in Beta

In this section we present a final modification of the model for tender offer firms which allows for the possibility that the beta coefficients are affected by the repurchase. A change in beta could be hypothesized based on either an increased use of leverage (beta increases) or perceived risk falling due to an information content to the repurchase announcement.

$$R_{it}{}^* = a_i + b_i R_{mt}{}^* + s_i S_{it} + d_i D_{it} + e_{it} \qquad (6.5)$$

where

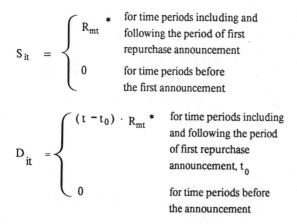

$$S_{it} = \begin{cases} R_{mt}{}^* & \text{for time periods including and following the period of first repurchase announcement} \\ 0 & \text{for time periods before the first announcement} \end{cases}$$

$$D_{it} = \begin{cases} (t - t_0) \cdot R_{mt}{}^* & \text{for time periods including and following the period of first repurchase announcement, } t_0 \\ 0 & \text{for time periods before the announcement} \end{cases}$$

and the other terms are as previously defined.

The coefficient of S_{it}, s_i, represents any shift in beta which occurs at or near the announcement period and is maintained thereafter. The coefficient of D_{it}, d_i, represents any trend in the beta coefficient after the repurchase. The inclusion of both the variables S_{it} and D_{it} in the model will allow us to determine whether any possible change in beta occurs

Table 6.8
RCR Estimates for Tender Offer Sample

Coefficient	Mean	Population Standard Deviation*	Test for mean Zero, t	Simultaneous Test Results Randomness, χ^2	Mean Zero, F

A. Subsequent Month and Month of Announcement Indicators

Coefficient	Mean	Pop. Std. Dev.*	t	χ^2	F
a_i	0.002	*	3.4		
b_i	1.070	0.312	26.5		
$C_{o;i}$	0.097	0.130	5.3		
$C_{+1;i}$	0.004	0.022	0.5		
$C_{+2;i}$	-0.008	0.027	-1.0		
$C_{+3;i}$	0.009	*	1.2	331.9	.8
$C_{+4;i}$	0.008	*	1.0		
$C_{+5;i}$	0.014	0.073	1.1		
$C_{+6;i}$	0.004	0.007	0.5		

1% critical value			2.6	333.7	3.1
Degrees of freedom			69	276	6,64

B. Prior Months and Month of Announcement Indicators

Coefficient	Mean	Pop. Std. Dev.*	t	χ^2	F
a_i	0.003	*	3.7		
b_i	1.070	0.307	26.9		
$C_{o;i}$	0.097	0.129	5.3		
$C_{-1;i}$	0.013	*	1.7		
$C_{-2;i}$	0.014	*	1.8		2.0
$C_{-3;i}$	-0.003	*	-0.4		

1% critical value			2.6		4.1
Degrees of freedom			69		3,67

C. Final Model

Coefficient	Mean	Pop. Std. Dev.*	t	χ^2
a_i	0.003	*	4.0	
b_i	1.069	0.305	27.0	556.0
$C_{o;i}$	0.097	0.130	5.3	211.6

1% critical value			2.6	99.3
Degrees of freedom			69	69

*Coefficients constrained to be fixed (i.e., those with zero variance restrictions imposed) are indicated by an asterisk (*).

Figure 6.2
Plot of Coefficient Means for Tender Offer Sample

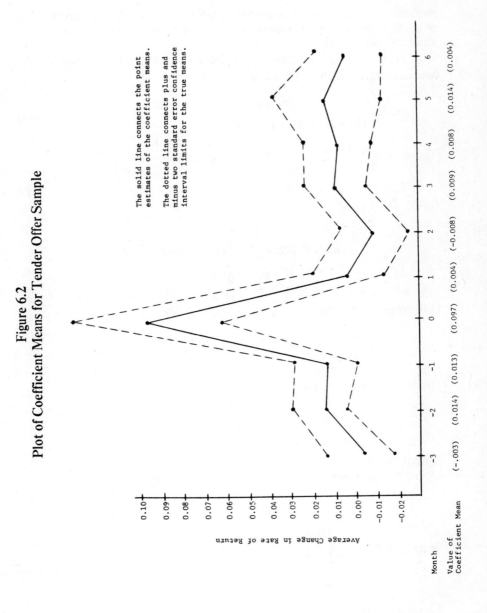

Pooled Data for Financial Markets

suddenly at the date of announcement (s_i significantly different from zero) or more slowly as a trend after the announcement (d_i significantly different from zero).

To better illustrate the use of these variables, we can think of the beta coefficient as having been decomposed into two parts:

$$
beta = \begin{cases} b_i & \text{before the first repurchase announcement} \\ b_i + s_i + d_i \cdot (t - t_0) & \text{for the time periods} \\ & \text{of and subsequent to} \\ & \text{the first announcement.} \end{cases} \quad (6.6)
$$

The 'beta' of each firm is therefore the sum of the effects accounted for by $R_{mt}*$.

Table 6.9
RCR Estimates for Tender Offer Sample

Coefficient	Mean	Population Standard Deviaion*	Test for Mean Zero, t	Test for Randomness, χ^2
A. Trend Versus Shift in Beta				
a_i	0.003	*	4.0	
b_i	1.169	0.357	24.3	
$C_{o;i}$	0.095	0.136	5.1	
S_i	-0.161	0.285	-3.1	110.92
d_i	-0.001	*	-1.4	
1% critical value			2.6	99.3
Degrees of freedom			69	69
B. Final Model				
a_i	0.003	*	4.0	
b_i	1.168	0.357	24.3	
$C_{o;i}$	0.095	0.129	5.2	204.8
S_i	-0.187	0.245	-4.4	138.8
1% critical value			2.6	99.3
Degrees of freedom			69	69

*Coefficients constrained to be fixed (i.e., those with zero variance restrictions imposed) are indicated by an asterisk (*).

The results of this analysis are presented in Panels A and B of Table 6.9.

In Panel A we find that the trend coefficient is fixed (due to a negative variance estimate) and is not significantly different from zero. We therefore omit the variable D_{it} from our model to obtain the results of our final model in Panel B. Here we see that the shift coefficient, S_i, has a mean that is significantly less than zero. We also note that the coefficient is random (population standard deviation is 0.245). Thus, although the effect on beta was not uniform across the sample, on average the information content of the repurchase announcement significantly reduced the market's perception of the firms' risk. This is indicated in the average drop of 0.187 in the beta coefficient. Note also that our earlier conclusions regarding the average positive price effects and the randomness of those effects are unchanged.

Section 6.13 Conclusions

Using a (mixed) random coefficient regression model to investigate the effects of stock repurchasing on rates of return and risk led to the following results:

1. Open market repurchases have no economic significance in the sense that the repurchase effects on rates of return are uniformly negligible.
2. Tender offer repurchases do not have a uniform effect on either the rate of return or on the beta, although, on the average, the repurchase is associate with significant increases in return in the month of the announcement and significant decreases in beta.
3. For tender offer repurchases, no significant effects on return were found in any month around the announcement date except during the announcement month itself. Thus, we find no evidence that leakage of information prior to the announcement affects the rate of return. Nor do we find that increases in rate of return during the annoucement month are offset when the tender offer terminates.

Section 6.14 Suggestions for Further Research

The results presented in this chapter suggest several additional avenues of research. The most immediate of these is an investigation of possible explanations for the differences in results between open market and tender offer firms and an investigation of variations in the effect on returns for firms repurchasing by tender offer.

The differences in results between tender offer and open market firms may be related to the size of repurchase. On the average, the open market repurchases are considerably smaller in terms of percentage than the tender offer repurchases.

The variation in the effect on returns and risk for stocks in the tender offer sample may possibly be explained by differing motivations for repurchasing the stock. The RCR method used throughout Chapter 6 would seem well suited to investigate the significance of any variables which could be used to characterize differing motivations in explaining such variation. There is a methodological problem with the technique that limits the effectiveness of such an extension of this research, however.[19] A solution to this problem will also be attempted in future research.

Beyond the empirical examination of repurchasing firms there are two main areas of study concerning RCR models that are suggested. First, the lack of knowledge of small sample behavior of the estimators and test statistics used has been pointed out. Simulation studies could be useful to provide information about this behavior and to compare the quality of estimates from the various models discussed in Chapters 2 and 5 under different sets of conditions. Secondly, reference was made to RCR models which include not only variation in coefficients across individual units but over time as well (see, for example, Hsiao, 1974, and Rosenberg, 1973a,b,c). Further investigation of such models and an examination of their usefulness in analyzing pooled cross-sectional and time series data is another subject for future research.

Appendix A

An Examination of Residual Analysis and a Possible Alternative

In Section A.1 of this appendix we present an example of how residual analysis might be used to determine the effect on rate of return of an announcement or release of information. The limitations of this approach are pointed out in Section A.2.

In Section A.3 we suggest an alternative to residual analysis which provides us with the least square estimate of the change in rate of return in the time period in which the announcement occurred. Since the intent of this research has been to provide methods which can assess overall market effects of such announcements (i.e., to provide the tools for statistical inference about the population of firms) we investigate methods of combining these separate equation least squares estimates to obtain an estimate of the mean or overall change in rate of return. As suggested by the pooling methodologies in Chapter 2, there are better approaches than this for both estimation and inference. We provide the example in this appendix to compare the use of a dummy variable or linear model approach to residual analysis, and to suggest a need to extend analytical capabilities beyond separate equation regression models to pooled cross-sectional and time series data models.

Section A.1: Residual Analysis

The Market Model

$$R_{it} = a_i + b_i R_{mt} + e_{it} \tag{A.1}$$

$$i = 1, \ldots, N$$

Assumptions

(1) One set of assumptions usually made is that the disturbance terms for the ith firm come from a distribution with mean O and variance σ_i^2:

$$E(e_{it}) = 0 \tag{A.2}$$

$$Var(e_{it}) = \sigma_i^2$$

Through the use of residual analysis, however, we implicitly assume that a new parameter (or parameters) is involved. Suppose there is an announcement of information in time period t_i for firm i. If we believe there may be a change in rate of return as a result of this announcement our original assumptions would be modified as follows:

$$E (e_{it}) = 0 \qquad \text{for } t \neq t_i$$
$$E (e_{it_i}) = e_i^* \qquad \text{for } t = t_i \qquad \qquad (A.3)$$
$$Var (e_{it}) = \sigma_i^2 \qquad \text{for all } t.$$

The new parameter e_i^* represents any unusual shift in return in period t_i plus any random movement attributed to chance.

(2)   There is no serial correlation present in the time series residuals:

$$E (e_{it} \; e_{it'}) = 0 \text{ for } t \neq t '. \qquad \qquad (A.4)$$

(3)   There is no contemporaneous correlation present in the residuals:

$$E (e_{it} \; e_{jt}) = 0 \text{ for } i \neq j. \qquad \qquad (A.5)$$

Estimation

The parameters of the market model are estimated using OLS. The estimates of a_i and b_i will be denoted $\hat{a}_i$ and $\hat{b}_i$, respectively.

We now calculate sample residuals

$$\hat{e}_{it} = R_{it} - \hat{R}_{it} \qquad \qquad (A.6)$$

where $\hat{R}_{it} = \hat{a}_i + \hat{b}_i \; R_{mt}$

Since we cannot observe the true residuals, e_{it}, we use the estimates, $\hat{e}_{it}$, as substitutes. In the time period of interest, t_i, we have $\hat{e}_i^* = R_{it_i} - \hat{R}_{it_i}$. We calculate the average residual for the sample of N firms from this time period as

$$\bar{e}^* = \frac{1}{N} \sum_{i=1}^{N} \hat{e}_i^* \qquad \qquad (A.7)$$

The sample variance is given by

$$S^2 = \frac{1}{N-1} \sum_{i=1}^{N} (\hat{e}_i^* - \bar{\hat{e}}^*)^2 \ . \tag{A.8}$$

Hypothesis

The hypothesis we wish to test is

$$H_0: \bar{e}^* = 0 \tag{A.9}$$

$$vs \ H_a: \bar{e}^* \neq 0$$

with level of significance α, where $\bar{e}^*$ is the population mean of the residuals in the period of announcement $(E(e_i^*) = \bar{e}^*)$.

Test Construction

The statistic often used is

$$T^* = \frac{\sqrt{N} \ \bar{\hat{e}}^*}{S} \ . \tag{A.10}$$

The statistic T^* will have (approximately) the t-distribution with N-1 degrees of freedom under the null hypothesis. We can state the critical region for our test as:

Reject H_0 if
$T^* > t_{\alpha/2, N-1}$
or $T^* < - t_{\alpha/2, N-1}$

where $t_{\alpha/2, \ N-1}$ is the appropriate value from a t-table with level of significance equal to α and with N-1 degrees of freedom.[1]

To justify the use of T^* we take a general sampling point of view and assume the N residuals from the time period of announcement come from a distribution with zero mean and variance, ∂:

$$e_i^* \sim iid \ (0, \partial).$$

We must work with estimates, $\hat{e}_i^*$, of the true e_i^*, however. We write these estimates as

$$\hat{e}_i^* = e_i^* + \text{error} \qquad\qquad (A.11)$$

where both e_i^* and the error are random with

$$E(e_i^*) = \bar{e},^* \qquad\qquad (A.12)$$
$$E(\text{error}) = 0.$$

This adds an additional component of variance that is independent of e_i^*. Writing σ^2 as the total variance of $\hat{e}_i^*$ we have

$$\hat{e}_i^* \sim \text{iid}\,(0, \sigma^2).$$

For large values of N the Central Limit Theorem applies and the sampling distribution of $\hat{e}^*$ can be determined:

$\bar{e}^*$ is approximately $N\,(\bar{e}^*, \sigma/\sqrt{N}\,)$.

It follows that

$$N^* = \frac{\sqrt{N}\,\bar{\hat{e}}^*}{\sigma} \sim N(0,1) \qquad\qquad (A.13)$$

under the null hypothesis in (A.9). Equation (A.10) follows using our estimate, $S = \sqrt{S^2}$, in place of σ.

Section A.2 Limitations of Residual Analysis

In the construction of the test statistic in equation (A.10) we first assume that the true residuals for firm i are drawn from a distribution with mean as given in (A.3) and variance σ_i^2. An unbiased estimate of this variance is obtained by using the mean square error from the ith separate regression:

$$\hat{\sigma}_i^2 = \frac{\sum_{t=1}^{T} (R_{it} - \hat{R}_{it})^2}{T - 2} \qquad\qquad (A.14)$$

We obtain the residuals for each announcement period and construct the t-statistic in equation (A.10). In the construction of this statistic we are implicitly assuming that the residuals from time period t_i are drawn from some distribution with mean $\bar{e}^*$ estimated by $\bar{\hat{e}}^*$ in (A.7) and variance σ^2 estimated by S^2 in (A.8). Our sampling approach disregards the original assumptions made about the e_{it}. If we were to use these assumptions we would have to view the e_{it_i} ($i=1, \ldots, N$) as random draws from distributions with variances that might differ. The estimates of these differing variances, the $\hat{\sigma}_i^2$ would have to be used in the construction of our statistic thus complicating matters considerably.

The procedure followed in residual analysis is similar to a technique referred to as "stagewise regression" by Draper and Smith (1966, pp. 173-77). In the first stage we perform a regression of our dependent variable, R_{it}, on an independent variable R_{mt}, and obtain the residuals. The second stage consists of regressing the residuals from the first stage against some independent variable which is correlated with the residuals. At each stage, the regression equations can be back-substituted stage by stage until the final stagewise solution is obtained. In residual analysis, the use of the residual in time period t_i as an estimate of the parameter e_i^* is equivalent to regressing the $\hat{e}_{it}$ on a $(0, 1)$ dummy variable which is equal to one in time period t_i.[2] As Draper and Smith point out, this approach does not provide the least square solution that would be obtained from the coefficient of the dummy variable in a multiple regression of R_{it} on R_{mt} and the dummy variable. The stagewise regression estimate, i.e. the residual itself, is smaller in absolute value than the least squares estimate of the coefficient of the dummy variable. Thus, use of the residuals might de-emphasize the amount that return is affected by the announcement.[3]

A further problem with the residual analysis approach is alluded to in the text of Chapter 2. There is no theoretical base for tests of many simultaneous hypotheses. This is to be expected since the theory pertaining to the very basic hypothesis suggested in this appendix is so sketchy.

Thus, although residual analysis has helped to shed light on the answers to several financial questions, the methodology is not without its limitations.

Section A.3 The Linear Model or Dummy Variable Approach

We again face the problem of determining whether an announcement of information in time period t_i has caused an unusual change in rate of return. We are interested not in the change for a paricular firm but in the overall change for the market.

The Amended Market Model

We add to the market model of (A.1) the variable $Z_{0;it}$ defined as

$$Z_{0;it} = \begin{cases} 1 \text{ in time period } t_i \\ 0 \text{ otherwise} \end{cases}$$

$i = 1, \ldots, N$

to obtain

$$R_{it} = a_i + b_i R_{mt} + c_{o,i} Z_{0;it} + e_{it}^4 \qquad (A.15)$$

Assumptions:

The assumptions are nearly identical to those made for residual analysis:

(1) $E(e_{it}) = 0^2$.
    $Var(e_{it}) = \sigma_i^2$.   (A.16)
(2) $E(e_{it} e_{it'}) = 0$ for $t \neq t'$.

(3) $E(e_{it} e_{jt}) = 0$ for $i \neq j$.

Estimation:

Estimates of a_i, b_i and $c_{o,i}$ are obtained by OLS and are denoted $\hat{a}_i$, $\hat{b}_i$ and $\hat{c}_{o,i}$ respectively. The variances of $\hat{a}_i$, $\hat{b}_i$ and $\hat{c}_{o,i}$ are estimated and denoted $\hat{V}(\hat{a}_i)$, $\hat{V}(\hat{b}_i)$ and $\hat{V}(\hat{c}_{o,i})$.

Hypotheses About Individual Firms

The linear model approach allows us to easily test hypotheses about the effect of a repurchase announcement on rate of return for individual firms:

$$H_o: c_{o,i} = 0 \qquad (A.17)$$

$$H_a: c_{o,i} \neq 0.$$

Most packaged regression programs automatically perform such tests.

Hypothesis About the Overall Effect

Our main concern is in making inferences about the population mean effect on rate of return. Denoting the population mean by c our hypothesis can be stated as

$$H_o: \bar{c} = 0$$

$$H_a: \bar{c} \neq 0 \tag{A.18}$$

with level significance $\alpha(E(c_{oi}) = \bar{c})$.

Test Construction

We can proceed as we did in residual analysis using a sampling approach. The $c_{o,i}$ are viewed as random drawings from a distribution with mean $\bar{c} = 0$ and variance δ:

$$c_{o,i} \sim iid\,(0, \delta).$$

Estimates, $\hat{c}_{o,i}$, are used in place of the true $c_{o,i}$ thus adding an additional component of variance:

$$\hat{c}_{o,i} = c_{o,i} + error \tag{A.19}$$

where $E(c_{o,i}) = \bar{c} = 0,$ $\tag{A.20}$

$$E\,(error) = 0.$$

If we let σ^2 denote the total variance we can write

$$\hat{c}_{o,i} \sim iid\,(0,\ \sigma^2).$$

$$\tag{A.21}$$

Using $\quad \hat{\bar{c}} = \dfrac{1}{N} \sum_{i=1}^{N} \hat{c}_{o,i}$

as an estimate of $\bar{c}$ and

$$s^2 = \frac{1}{N-1} \sum_{i=1}^{N} (\hat{c}_{o,i} - \hat{\bar{c}})^{2} \tag{A.22}$$

as an estimate of σ^2 we construct the statistic

$$T = \frac{\sqrt{N} \; \hat{\bar{c}}}{S} \tag{A.23}$$

which has (approximately) a t-distribution with N-1 degrees of freedom under the null hypothesis in (A.18). The critical region for our test can be stated as:

Reject H_o if

$$T > t_{\alpha/2, \, N-1}$$

or $T < -t_{\alpha/2, \, N-1}$

where $t_{\alpha/2, \, N-1}$ is the tabled t-value for level of significance α and N-1 degrees of freedom.[5]

Section A.4 Summary

The linear model approach goes beyond stagewise regression to obtain the least squares estimate of individual announcement effects. Using this approach provides a convenient method of testing the significance of effects for individual firms using the t-statistic normally calculated in regression output. We also have the capability of testing simultaneous hypotheses for individual firms. Our main goal, however, is to test the significance of the overall or market effect of an announcement. The linear model approach does provide us with standard errors of the estimates of announcement effects for individual firms. We have not, however, used these estimates in constructing the t-statistic for the test of our overall hypothesis. This approach would lead to a very complicated test procedure. Theoretically, then, the linear model approach is not as elegant as we would like it to be. It overcomes certain limitations of residual analysis by allowing us to perform tests on individual firm effects and simultaneous tests on several coefficients for individual firms. But our test of the overall hypothesis is not much of an improvement over the residual analysis procedure.

In Chapter 2 we incorporate the idea of using dummy variables to examine repurchase announcement effects into models especially designed for pooled cross-sectional and time series data. Direct inference about population parameters is provided by certain of these models. Statistics in these cases are theoretically more appealing than the measures used by residual analysis (Equation A.10) and the linear model method (Equation A.23). Models such as Swamy's RCR model are seen to be feasible possibilities in financial analyses such as our analysis of repurchase announcement effects.

Appendix B

A Review of Small Sample Properties
For the SUR and RCR Models

We review here the current knowledge of small sample properties for the SUR and RCR models.

Section B.1 Seemingly Unrelated Regressions

The small sample properties of Zellner's estimation (ZEF) were first investigated by Zellner and Huang (1962) and Zellner (1963). They showed that the gain in efficiency from using Zellner's SUR approach rather than separate equation regressions (SER) is affected by relationships between the explanatory variables as well as the magnitude of the contemporaneous correlation. Recently, Swamy and Metha (1976) presented a derivation of the exact second moments of Zellner's estimator for a two equation system. They found that the conditions under which ZEF provides a definite gain in efficiency over SER are:

(1) $|\rho| \geq .3$, where ρ is the contemporaneous correlation coefficient, and
(2) $T \geq K + 23$, where K is the number of explanatory variables.

Srivastava (1970) attempted a similar analysis in a general system of more than two equations. His approximate second-order moment matrix is so complicated, however, that it precludes deduction of any definite conclusions concerning small sample properties.

In terms of bias, Kakwani (1967) has shown that the ZEF estimator is unbiased, in general, provided its mean exists and the disturbances follow a continuous symmetric probability law.

Kmenta and Gilbert (1968) investigated the small sample properties of several estimators of seemingly unrelated regressions via Monte Carlo simulations. The alternative estimators included:

(1) Separate equation regressions (SER)
(2) Zellner's two-stage Aitken procedure (ZEF)
(3) Zellner's iterative Aitken procedure (IZEF)

(4) Telser's iterative procedure (TIE)
(5) Maximum likelihood estimation (ML).

For samples of 10, 20 and 100 and various model specifications they found that IZEF, TIE and ML lead to identical coefficient estimates. The results, in general, however, favor the ZEF over the other estimators. ZEF is more efficient than SER even in small samples and performs as well, on average, as the other procedures. Kmenta and Gilbert suggest that, considering their results, ZEF is likely to be preferred to IZEF, TIE and ML since these latter three procedures are considerably more time consuming.

Parks (1967) proposed an extension of the ZEF technique to handle those cases when both auto and contemporaneous correlation of residuals are present. The small sample properties of this procedure were investigated by Kmenta and Gilbert (1970) and compared to several alternative approaches. Although the Parks procedure was computationally simpler, they found a nonlinear procedure which provides joint estimates of the regression coefficients and autocorrelation coefficients to provide, on average, the best results. Their criteria for ranking the estimation techniques examined were as follows:

(1) smaller standard deviations of the regression coefficient
(2) smaller root mean squared error for estimates of the auto-correlation coefficient.

The joint nonlinear technique mentioned previously performed as well or better than other techniques examined for both the criteria.

Section B.2 The RCR Model

Little has been published regarding the examination of small sample properties of random coefficient techniques. Although the estimators and inferential procedures are justified asymptotically, their behavior in small samples is virtually unknown. The researcher involved in the use of the RCR model must, therefore, be wary of results obtained when his time series involve only a few observations. (The asymptotic properties of the RCR procedures assume $T \rightarrow \infty$ where T = number of time series observations. Exactly how big T must be in order to constitute a "large" sample is questionable and must be determined by the researcher.)

One available simulation study by Johnson Lyon (1973) investigates alternative estimators in dynamic models (i.e., models with a lagged value of the dependent variable as an explanatory variable).

Their results indicate that Swamy's RCR approach may perform rather poorly in these dynamic models. Coefficient estimators were compared on the basis of bias. The poor performance of Swamy's model in this simulation is not unexpected, however. Swamy (1971, p. 143) himself points out the cautions of using the RCR approach when lagged values of the dependent variable are used as explanatory variables.

No simulation studies are known to this author involving the RCR model when no lagged variables are involved. As mentioned, the estimation techniques and hypothesis tests for the RCR and mixed RCR models are justified on asymptotic grounds only. As the use of these procedures becomes more common, investigation of small sample behavior will provide further guidelines for appropriate use of the methods.

Appendix C

Mathematical Presentation of The Mixed RCR Model

In this appendix we provide the reader with a mathematical presentation of the mixed random coefficient regression model. Many of the results presented here are due to Swamy (1971, pp. 143-55); their inclusion here is simply to save the interested reader from searching out the reference.

Section C.1 The Mixed RCR Model

$$\underline{Y}_i = X_{1i} \underline{b}_{1i} + X_{2i} \underline{b}_2 + \underline{e}_i \tag{C.1}$$

$$i = 1, \ldots, N$$

where

$\underline{Y}_i$ is a $T \times 1$ vector of observations on the dependent variable;
X_{1i} and X_{2i} are $T \times K_1$ and $T \times K_2$ matrices, respectively, of observations on the independent variables;
$\underline{b}_{1i}$ is a $K_1 \times 1$ vector of random coefficients;
$\underline{b}_2$ is a $K_2 \times 1$ vector of fixed coefficients (we delete the subscript 'i' since the coefficients $\underline{b}_{2i}$ are equal for all individual units);
$\underline{e}_i$ is a $T \times 1$ vector of random disturbances.

Section C.2 Assumptions

(1) $T > K_1 + K_2$.
(2) The X_{1i} and X_{2i} are non-stochastic.
(3) rank $(X_{1i}) = K_1$.
    rank $(X_{2i}) = K_2$.
(4) The $\underline{b}_{1i}$ are iid with mean $\overline{\underline{b}}_1$ and variance-covariance matrix Δ_{b_1}.
(5) The $\underline{e}_i$ are independently distributed with
    $E(\underline{e}_i) = 0$
    $E(\underline{e}_i \underline{e}_i') = \sigma_i^2 I_T$
(6) The $\underline{b}_{1i}$ and $\underline{e}_j$ are independent for all i,j.

Appendix C

Section C.3 Estimation

Rewriting the $\underline{b}_{1i}$ as a fixed component plus a random component and substituting into (C.1) we have:

$$\underline{Y}_i = X_{1i}(\bar{\underline{b}}_1 + \underline{\delta}_i) + X_{2i}\underline{b}_2 + \underline{e}_i = X_{1i}\bar{\underline{b}}_1 + X_{2i}\underline{b}_2 + \underline{u}_i, \qquad \text{(C.2)}$$

$$i = 1, \ldots, N$$

where

$\underline{u}_i = X_{1i}\underline{\delta}_i + \underline{e}_i$ is a disturbance term consisting of all random components of the model and
the $\underline{\delta}_i$ are the random components of the coefficients $\underline{b}_{1i}$ with

$$E(\underline{\delta}_i) = 0$$

$$E(\underline{\delta}_i\underline{\delta}_i') = \Delta_{b_1}. \qquad \text{(C.3)}$$

We can write the set of all N equations given by (C.2) as

$$\underline{Y} = X_1\bar{\underline{b}}_1 + X_2\underline{b}_2 + \underline{U} \qquad \text{(C.4)}$$

where

$$\underline{Y} = \begin{bmatrix} \underline{Y}_1 \\ \underline{Y}_2 \\ \vdots \\ \underline{Y}_N \end{bmatrix}, \quad X_1 = \begin{bmatrix} X_{11} \\ X_{12} \\ \vdots \\ X_{1N} \end{bmatrix}, \quad X_2 = \begin{bmatrix} X_{21} \\ X_{22} \\ \vdots \\ X_{2N} \end{bmatrix} \qquad \text{(C.5)}$$

$$\underline{U} = \begin{bmatrix} X_{11} & 0 & - - - & 0 \\ 0 & X_{12} & & 0 \\ \vdots & \vdots & \ddots & \vdots \\ 0 & 0 & - - - & X_{1N} \end{bmatrix} \begin{bmatrix} \underline{\delta}_1 \\ \underline{\delta}_2 \\ \vdots \\ \underline{\delta}_N \end{bmatrix} + \begin{bmatrix} \underline{e}_1 \\ \underline{e}_2 \\ \vdots \\ \underline{e}_N \end{bmatrix} \qquad \text{(C.6)}$$

$$= D(X_1)\underline{\delta} + \underline{e} \qquad \text{(C.7)}$$

Equation (C.4) represents a linear regression model with non-spherical disturbance covariance matrix. The covariance matrix can be written

$$\Sigma = E(\underline{U}\,\underline{U}') \quad = \qquad\qquad\qquad\qquad\qquad\qquad (C.8)$$

$$= \begin{bmatrix} X_{11} \Delta_1 X'_{11} + \sigma_1^2 I_T & 0 & \text{-----------} & 0 \\[2ex] 0 & X_{12} \Delta_1 X'_{12} + \sigma_2^2 I_T & \text{----} & 0 \\[2ex] 0 & 0 & \text{----} \; X_{1N} \Delta_1 X'_{1N} + \sigma_N^2 I_T \end{bmatrix}$$

where

the I_T represent $T \times T$ identity matrices, and the 0's are $T \times T$ null matrices.

Once again rewrite the model last given by (C.4) as

$$Y = X \underline{b} + \underline{u} \qquad\qquad\qquad\qquad\qquad\qquad (C.9)$$

where

$$X = \begin{bmatrix} \overline{X}_1 \\ \overline{X}_2 \\ \vdots \\ \overline{X}_N \end{bmatrix} = \begin{bmatrix} X_{11} & X_{21} \\ X_{12} & X_{22} \\ \vdots & \vdots \\ X_{1N} & X_{2N} \end{bmatrix} \quad \text{and} \qquad (C.10)$$

$$\underline{b} = \begin{bmatrix} \underline{b}_1 \\ \underline{b}_2 \end{bmatrix} \cdot \qquad\qquad\qquad\qquad\qquad\qquad (C.11)$$

Since (C.9) is a linear model with non-spherical disturbance covariance matrix, Σ, the best linear unbiased estimate of $\underline{b}$ is given by the generalized least squares estimator:

$$\tilde{\underline{b}} = \begin{bmatrix} \tilde{\underline{b}}_1 \\ \tilde{\underline{b}}_2 \end{bmatrix} = (X' \Sigma^{-1} X)^{-1} (X' \Sigma^{-1} Y) \tag{C.12}$$

which can be shown to simplify to $\hspace{8cm}$ (C.13)

$$\tilde{\underline{b}} = \left[\sum_{j=1}^{N} \left\{ \Delta_{b_1} + \sigma_j^2 (\overline{X}_j'\overline{X}_j)^{-1} \right\}^{-1} \right]^{-1} \sum_{i=1}^{N} [\Delta_{b_1} + \sigma_i^2(\overline{X}_i'\overline{X}_i)^{-1}]^{-1} \hat{\underline{b}}_i$$

where

$$\hat{\underline{b}}_i = (\overline{X}_i'\overline{X}_i)^{-1}\overline{X}_i'\underline{Y}_i \tag{C.14}$$

and the $\overline{X}_i$ are as given in (C.10) for $i=1, \ldots, N$.

Before equation (C.13) can be applied in practice we must obtain estimates of the parameters Δ_{b_1}, $\sigma_1^2, \sigma_2^2, \ldots, \sigma_N^2$. If we replace these parameters by consistent estimates, say, $\hat{\Delta}_{b_1}$, $\hat{\sigma}_1^2, \ldots, \hat{\sigma}_N^2$, we insure that the new estimator, $\hat{\underline{b}}$ will be a consistent and asymptotically efficient estimate of $\underline{b}$ (Swamy, 1971, pp. 144-46).

We now have $\hspace{9cm}$ (C.15)

$$\hat{\underline{b}} = \left[\sum_{j=1}^{N} \left\{ \hat{\Delta}_{b_1} + \hat{\sigma}_j^2 (\overline{X}_j'\overline{X}_j)^{-1} \right\}^{-1} \right]^{-1} \cdot \sum_{i=1}^{N} [\hat{\Delta}_{b_1} + \hat{\sigma}_i^2(\overline{X}_i'\overline{X}_i)^{-1}]^{-1} \hat{\underline{b}}_i$$

Consistent estimators of the $\hat{\sigma}_j^2$ are given by

$$\hat{\sigma}_j^2 = \frac{\underline{Y}_i' M_i \underline{Y}_i}{T - K_1 - K_2} \tag{C.16}$$

where

$$M_i = I_T - \overline{X}_i(\overline{X}_i'\overline{X}_i)^{-1}\overline{X}_i' . \tag{C.17}$$

A consistent estimator of Δ_{b_1} is given by

$$\hat{\Delta}_{b_1} = \frac{S_{b_1}}{N-1} - \frac{1}{N} \sum_{i=1}^{N} \hat{\sigma}_i^2 \; (\bar{X}_i' \, \bar{X}_i)_*^{-1} \tag{C.18}$$

where

$$S_{b_1} = \sum_{i=1}^{N} \hat{\underline{b}}_{1i} \, \hat{\underline{b}}_{1i}' - \frac{1}{N} \sum_{i=1}^{N} \hat{\underline{b}}_{1i} \sum_{i=1}^{N} \hat{\underline{b}}_{1i}' \; , \tag{C.19}$$

$\hat{\underline{b}}_{1i}$ is the OLS estimate of $\underline{b}_{1i}$ for equation (C.1), and $(\bar{X}_i' \, \bar{X}_i)_*^{-1}$ denotes the upper left hand K_1 x K_1 partition of the matrix

$$(\bar{X}_i' \, \bar{X}_i)^{-1} = \begin{bmatrix} X_{1i}' \, X_{1i} & X_{2i}' \, X_{1i} \\[2ex] X_{1i}' \, X_{2i} & X_{2i}' \, X_{2i} \end{bmatrix}^{-1} . \tag{C.20}$$

Note further that the estimated variance-covariance matrix of the estimator, $\hat{\underline{b}}$, is given by

$$V(\hat{\underline{b}}) = \left[\sum_{j=1}^{N} \left\{ \hat{\Delta}_{b_1} + \hat{\sigma}_j^2 \; (\bar{X}_j' \, \bar{X}_j)^{-1} \right\}^{-1} \right]^{-1} . \tag{C.21}$$

Thus, to obtain standard errors of estimates for use in the construction of statistics and confidence intervals we use the square roots of appropriate diagonal elements of $V(\hat{\underline{b}})$.

Section C.4 Existing Tests of Hypotheses

The following is a survey of existing hypothesis tests for the mixed RCR model.

(1) A test for the full mean vector of random coefficients.

Rewriting (C.4), with $\underline{b}_2$ assumed equal to zero, as

$$\underline{Y} = X_i \bar{\underline{b}}_1 + \underline{u} \tag{C.22}$$

we find that Swamy presents a test of the hypothesis

$$H_o: \bar{\underline{b}}_1 = \bar{\underline{b}}_{10} \tag{C.23}$$

where $\bar{\underline{b}}_{10}$ is a vector of preassigned values. Note that this model includes only those coefficients assumed to be random. The test statistic is given by

$$\frac{N - K_1}{K_1(N-1)} (\hat{\underline{b}}_1 - \bar{\underline{b}}_{10})' \, V(\hat{\underline{b}}_1)^{-1} (\hat{\underline{b}}_1 - \bar{\underline{b}}_{10}) \tag{C.24}$$

which is asymptotically distributed as F with K_1 and N-K_1 degrees of freedom (see Swamy, 1971, pp. 121-22) under the null hypothesis in (C.23).

Swamy (1971, pp. 120-21) has also developed an asymptotic t-statistic to test hypotheses about a single coefficient mean.[1]

(2) A test for randomness of coefficients.

Using the model given in (C.1) Swamy presents a test of the hypothesis

$$H_o: \Delta_{b_1} = 0 \text{ given } E(\underline{b}_{1i}) = \bar{\underline{b}}_1$$

for all $i = 1, \ldots, N$. (C.25)

A synonym for the word "given" in the above hypothesis might be "assuming." Swamy is assuming that the coefficients $\underline{b}_{1i}$, if random, are all from a distribution with common mean. If, however, the hypothesis $\Delta_{b_1} = 0$ is accepted, the condition $E(\underline{b}_{1i}) \, \bar{\underline{b}}_1$ means that the coefficients are not only non-random but are equal ($\underline{b}_{11} = \underline{b}_{12} = \ldots = b_{1N}$) for all N individuals. This is especially important in Swamy's presentation of the test since he makes a distinction between coefficients that are fixed (non-random) and equal for all individuals and coefficients that are fixed but differ from one individual to another. The concept of fixed but different coefficients is more appealing to many researchers than the idea of random coefficients, but in order to support inference from sample to population, we will deal with fixed coefficients only as those coefficients that are equal for all individual units in our analysis. This is indicated in our notation by writing $\underline{b}_2$ (rather than $\underline{b}_{2i}$ as Swamy might use) to represent a coefficient assumed fixed across N individual units.

The development of the test statistic for the hypothesis in (C.25) is through use of the likelihood ratio (LR) criterion.

The statistic is given by

$$\hat{\lambda} = \frac{\displaystyle\prod_{i=1}^{N} S_i^{-T}}{\displaystyle\prod_{i=1}^{N} \left\{ \hat{\sigma}_i^{-(T-K_1)} \mid X_{1i}' X_{1i} \mid^{-1/2} \mid \frac{1}{N} S_{b_1} \mid^{-1/2} \right\}} \tag{C.26}$$

where

S_i^2 is the exact maximum likelihood estimate of σ_i^2 under H_o,
$\hat{\sigma}_i^2$ is given in (C.16) and S_{b_1} is given in (C.19).

The statistic $\hat{\lambda}$ is not an exact LR statistic since the estimators in (C.16) and (C.19) are not true maximum likelihood (ML) estimators.[2] They are asymptotically equivalent to their corresponding ML estimators which means that, asymptotically, $-2\ln\hat{\lambda}$ will have the same distribution as $-2\ln\lambda$ where λ is the LR statistic if exact ML estimates are used. This distribution is χ^2 with $\frac{1}{2} K_1(K_1 + 1)$ degrees of freedom.

(3) A test of equality of coefficients (or, an indirect test of randomness).

Rewriting (C.1), with $\underline{b}_2$ assumed equal to zero, as

$$\underline{Y}_i = X_{1i}\underline{b}_{1i} + \underline{e}_i \tag{C.27}$$

and assuming the $\underline{b}_{1i}$ to be non-random, Swamy extends a test developed by Zellner (1962) to test the following hypothesis:

$$H_0: \underline{b}_{11} = \underline{b}_{12} = \ldots = \underline{b}_{1N} = \underline{b}_1 \tag{C.28}$$

$$\text{given } \Delta_{b_1} = 0$$

$$\text{vs } H_a: \underline{b}_{11} \neq \underline{b}_{12} \neq \ldots \neq \underline{b}_{1N}$$

We do not actually test any assumption about Δ_{b_1}; we test whether the coefficient vectors are equal for all N individual units. Since this is consistent with our definition of fixed vs. random coefficients, the test can be (and often is) used as an indirect means of testing for randomness of coefficients. This test is commonly used in practice rather than the test developed in the previous section, probably due to the relative computational ease of the indirect test.

The test statistic in this instance is given by

$$\sum_{i=1}^{N} \frac{(\hat{\underline{b}}_{1i} - \hat{\underline{b}}_1)' X'_{1i} X_{1i} (\hat{\underline{b}}_{1i} - \hat{\underline{b}}_1)}{\hat{\sigma}_i^{\ 2}} \tag{C.29}$$

which is asymptotically distributed as χ^2 with $K_1(N - 1)$ degrees of freedom. Notation in (C.29) is as follows:

$\hat{\underline{b}}_{1i} = (X'_{1i}X_{1i})^{-1}X'_{1i}\underline{Y}_i$;

$\hat{\sigma}_i^{\ 2}$ = the mean square error from the ith individual regression;

$\hat{\underline{b}}_1$ = classical pooled regression estimate obtained under the assumptions of H_o.

Appendix D

Simulation Study of
Two Tests for Randomness of Coefficients

To aid in deciding whether to use an indirect test for randomness of coefficients, or a test statistic which is asymptotically equivalent to the LR test statistic, a simulation experiment was performed. Although certainly not an exhaustive study, the results strongly suggest that the indirect test will outperform the LR equivalent test. The two tests are described in detail in Appendix C and an extension of the indirect test is suggested in Chapter 3.

Section D. 1 The Model

$$Y_{it} = a_i + b_i X_{it} + e_{it} \qquad\qquad (D.1)$$

$$i = 1, \ldots, 10$$

$$t = 1, \ldots, 50$$

Section D. 2 Generation of Data

Fifty time series observations of the independent variable, X_{it}, were generated for each of ten firms.[1] The coefficients a_i and b_i were either assigned fixed values or generated as random draws from normal distributions depending on the model examined. Normal random disturbances, e_{it}, were also generated. The dependent variable, Y_{it}, was calculated as the linear combination of a_i, $b_i X_{it}$ and e_{it} shown in equation (D.1). This procedure was used to generate data for 16 different models.

The data generated is summarized in the following three tables. Note that we have used four models with both coefficients fixed, four with both coefficients random and eight models with both a fixed and a random coefficient.

Table D.1
Fixed Coefficient Models

Model Number	a	b	X	e
1	2.0	10.0	N(40.0,25.0)	N(0.0,25.0)
2	2.0	10.0	N(40.0,25.0)	N(0.0, 4.0)
3	0.03	1.0	N(2.0, 5.0)	N(0.0, 2.0)
4	0.03	1.0	N(2.0, 5.0)	N(0.0, 1.0)

Table D.2
Random Coefficient Models

Model Number	a	b	X	e
5	N(2.0, 0.25)	N(10.0,2.25)	N(40.0,25.0)	N(0.0,25.0)
6	N(2.0, 0.25)	N(10.0,2.25)	N(40.0,25.0)	N(0.0, 4.0)
7	N(0.03,0.0001)	N(1.0,0.01)	N(2.0, 5.0)	N(0.0, 2.0)
8	N(0.03,0.0001)	N(1.0,0.01)	N(2.0, 5.0)	N(0.0, 1.0)

Table D.3
Mixed Models

Model Number	a	b	X	e
9	N(2.0, 0.25)	10.0	N(40.0,25.0)	N(0.0,25.0)
10	N(2.0, 0.25)	10.0	N(40.0,25.0)	N(0.0, 4.0)
11	N(0.03,0.0001)	1.0	N(2.0, 5.0)	N(0.0, 2.0)
12	N(0.03,0.0001)	1.0	N(2.0, 5.0)	N(0.0, 1.0)
13	2.0	N(10.0,2.25)	N(40.0,25.0)	N(0.0,25.0)
14	2.0	N(10.0,2.25)	N(40.0,25.0)	N(0.0, 4.0)
15	0.03	N(1.0,0.01)	N(2.0, 5.0)	N(0.0, 2.0)
16	0.03	N(1.0,0.01)	N(2.0, 5.0)	N(0.0, 1.0)

Section D.3 Procedure

Each of the 16 models was estimated using Swamy's RCR approach under the assumption that both coefficients were random. Suggestions from the schema of Chapter 5 were used as a guideline to model specification. Any negative variance estimates were constrained to equal zero and these coefficients were considered fixed in re-estimation of the model. Both tests for randomness were used in an attempt to properly specify the model.

Section D.4 Results

Table D.4 shows which models were correctly and incorrectly specified by the two tests. The indirect test clearly outperforms the asymptotically equivalent LR test. This latter test consistently accepted the null hypothesis of non-randomness of coefficients in every case. Thus only the fixed coefficient models were correctly specified. The indirect test chose the correct specification in 10 out of the 16 models.

Table D.4
Comparison of the Two Tests

	Models Correctly Specified	Models Incorrectly Specified	Percent Correctly Specified
Indirect Test	1,2,3,4,7,8,11, 13,14,16	5,6,9,10,12,15	62.5%
LR Equivalent Test	1,2,3,4	5,6,7,8,9,10,11, 12,13,14,15,16	25.0%

Section D.5 Conclusion

The failure of the likelihood ratio test is discouraging but not totally unexpected. We are not calculating exact values of the likelihoods due to the complexity of this task. Asymptotically equivalent estimators are used in place of the maximum likelihood estimators. This fact may be in part to blame for the poor performance of this test. Even exact maximum likelihood techniques have fallen short of desired behavior in other pooled cross-sectional and time series data applications, however. For example, Nerlove (1971a) investigated their use with the error components model and found their performance to be very poor in comparison to other techniques.

Due to the poor performance of the LR equivalent test we suggest the use of the indirect test in determining whether coefficients are fixed or random. When exact ML techniques are available the performance of the LR test can be re-evaluated and a new decision based on the performance of the two tests can be made.

Appendix E

Graphical Presentation of
Initial OLS Coefficient Estimates

In Chapter 6 we analyzed the effects over a period of months of a stock repurchase announcement on the rates of return of a number of firms. The OLS coefficients from a number of linear regressions were calculated and used to obtain RCR model estimates of the means and variances of each coefficient.

Also useful in analyses such as those described in Chapter 6 is the graphical examination of the initial OLS coefficient estimates. In this appendix we supplement the Chapter 6 analyses with

(1) boxplots of the OLS coefficient estimates, and
(2) some simple descriptive statistics.

Examination of the boxplots can aid the researcher by providing him with a graphical comparison of

(1) the variation of the individual OLS coefficient estimates and
(2) the overall level of the estimates.

Notation for the boxplots is as follows

(1) The box itself represents the midspread of the data with the upper edge (hinge) equal to the third quartile and the lower edge (hinge) equal to the first quartile.
(2) The * is the median.
(3) If there are no data values greater than one midspread above the upper hinge an X will appear at the most extreme value. This is also true for the data falling below the lower hinge.
(4) Outliers between one and one half midspreads from the upper and lower hinges are marked by an O or an O_n where n equals the number of outliers falling at the same point.
(5) Outliers falling more than one and one half midspreads from the hinges are marked by @ or @n if there are multiple outliers at the same point.

The program used to calculate the appropriate statistics and draw the boxplots is a modified version of a program written by McNeil (1977). All modifications are due to the author.

The different sets of boxplots correspond to the model results presented in the tables of Chapter 6.

Section E.1   Information From Examination of Boxplots

The variation in the individual OLS coefficient estimates is easily seen in any set of boxplots. As an example, consider the boxplots in Figure E.1. The coefficients a_i obviously exhibit the least amount of variation from firm to firm and the b_i exhibit the greatest amount. The remaining coefficients, $C_{o;i}$ through $C_{+6;i}$ exhibit differing degrees of variation. From the RCR analysis of Chapter 6 we concluded that only the coefficients b_i, $C_{+4;i}$, $C_{+5;i}$ and $C_{+6;i}$ were significantly random. From our graphical analysis we might question whether the appearance of randomness in $C_{+4;i}$, $C_{+5;i}$ and $C_{+6;i}$ is due to the presence of outliers. A further investigation of the variation in these coefficients with emphasis on examining the effect of the outliers would prove useful. The randomness of these coefficients is especially interesting since financial theory suggests no reason for this occurrence.

In our RCR analysis of open market repuchases we also concluded that the average effect on return in the month of announcement and the six subsequent months was equal to zero. This conclusion is supported by the boxplots. The medians (*) of the coefficients, $C_{o;i}$ through $C_{+6;i}$ fall near zero and the individual coefficients are distributed in a fairly symmetric manner around zero.

Throughout the RCR analysis we assumed all random coefficients were normally distributed. This assumption was made to allow inferences from our sample to the population of all repurchasing firms. From the boxplots we note some asymmetry in the distributions of certain random coefficients which might lead us to question the normality assumption. Consider the boxplots in Figure E.6, for example. In our RCR analysis the constant, a, was determined to be fixed across all firms. Tests performed on the remaining coefficients indicated significant randomness, however.

The boxplot for the coefficients, $C_{o;i}$, which represent the month of announcement effect on return, has several outliers with relatively large positive values. It appears, therefore, that this distribution may deviate from normality perhaps due to a positively skewed population. The Lilliefors (1967) test for normality was performed in cases such as this and indicated that the hypothesis of a normally distributed population could not be rejected at the .01 level of significance.

As a final example of the use of boxplots we consider again Figure E.6 and the outliers present for the coefficients, $C_{o;i}$. Since these outliers represent stocks with unusually large increases in rate of return in the month of a stock repurchase announcement, the firms themselves may warrant further investigation. Perhaps we can isolate characteristics of these firms that are associated with such unusually large changes in return. This would provide additional information useful in the refinement of financial theory which attempts to describe pricing behavior when repurchases are announced.

Table E.1

Open Market Firms: Announcement and One to Six Month Subsequent Indicators

Coefficient	Maximum	Upper Quartile	Median	Lower Quartile	Minimum
a_i	0.013	0.006	0.003	-0.000	-0.008
b_i	2.757	1.170	0.906	0.751	0.381
$C_{o;i}$	0.329	0.064	0.013	-0.037	-0.192
$C_{+1;i}$	0.142	0.045	-0.008	-0.048	-0.235
$C_{+2;i}$	0.321	0.044	-0.009	-0.052	-0.172
$C_{+3;i}$	0.220	0.041	-0.002	-0.049	-0.212
$C_{+4;i}$	0.347	0.047	-0.004	-0.046	-0.200
$C_{+5;i}$	0.340	0.070	0.011	-0.032	-0.242
$C_{+6;i}$	0.309	0.034	-0.004	-0.039	-0.242

Table E.2
Open Market Firms: Significant Variables
From Previous Analysis Plus Three Prior Month Indicators

Coefficient	Maximum	Upper Quartile	Median	Lower Quartile	Minimum
a_i	0.012	0.006	0.003	-0.000	-0.008
b_i	2.716	1.175	0.910	0.750	0.373
$C_{o;i}$	0.332	0.063	0.011	-0.041	-0.191
$C_{+4;i}$	0.347	0.047	-0.008	-0.043	-0.201
$C_{+5;i}$	0.340	0.072	0.011	-0.031	-0.243
$C_{+6;i}$	0.304	0.034	-0.005	-0.039	-0.241
$C_{-1;i}$	0.250	0.035	-0.016	-0.065	-0.168
$C_{-2;i}$	0.195	0.032	0.000	-0.044	-0.224
$C_{-3;i}$	0.225	0.035	-0.007	-0.048	-0.220

Figure E.1
Open Market Firms: Announcement and One to Six Month
Subsequent Indicators (See Table 6.7, Panel A)

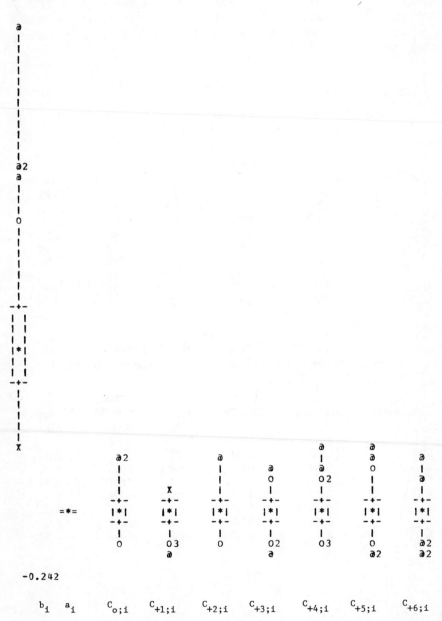

$$b_i \qquad a_i \qquad c_{o;i} \qquad c_{+1;i} \qquad c_{+2;i} \qquad c_{+3;i} \qquad c_{+4;i} \qquad c_{+5;i} \qquad c_{+6;i}$$

Figure E.2
Open Market Firms: Significant Variables
From Previous Analysis Plus Three Prior Month Indicators
(See Table 6.7, Panel B)

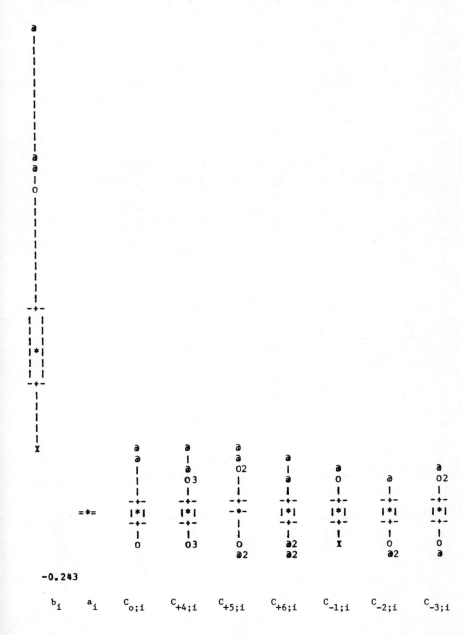

Table E.3
Tender Offer Firms: Announcement and One to Six Month Subsequent Indicators

Coefficient	Maximum	Upper Quartile	Median	Lower Quartile	Minimum
a_i	0.023	0.006	0.002	-0.001	-0.012
b_i	2.060	1.298	1.040	0.858	0.371
$C_{0;i}$	0.601	0.176	0.083	0.005	-0.167
$C_{+1;i}$	0.276	0.078	0.013	-0.038	-0.174
$C_{+2;i}$	0.351	0.047	-0.004	-0.058	-0.184
$C_{+3;i}$	0.253	0.057	0.014	-0.025	-0.180
$C_{+4;i}$	0.262	0.043	0.000	-0.034	-0.232
$C_{+5;i}$	0.428	0.068	0.010	-0.039	-0.361
$C_{+6;i}$	0.230	0.066	0.003	-0.038	-0.267

Table E.4
Tender Offer Firms: Significant Variables From Previous Analysis Plus Three Prior Month Indicators

Coefficient	Maximum	Upper Quartile	Median	Lower Quartile	Minimum
a_i	0.022	0.006	0.003	-0.001	0.018
b_i	2.014	1.310	1.044	0.838	0.385
$C_{0;i}$	0.604	0.167	0.083	0.003	-0.162
$C_{-1;i}$	0.157	0.065	0.012	-0.045	-0.254
$C_{-2;i}$	0.249	0.049	0.009	-0.041	-0.179
$C_{-3;i}$	0.209	0.030	-0.015	-0.052	-0.174

Table E.5
Tender Offer Firms: Final Model

Coefficient	Maximum	Upper Quartile	Median	Lower Quartile	Minimum
a_i	0.023	0.006	0.003	0.000	-0.019
b_i	2.027	1.294	1.047	0.852	0.400
$C_{0;i}$	0.605	0.167	0.083	0.003	-0.165

Table E.6
Tender Offer Firms: Change in Beta

Coefficient	Maximum	Upper Quartile	Median	Lower Quartile	Minimum
a_i	0.023	0.007	0.003	-0.000	-0.020
b_i	2.159	1.492	1.179	0.869	0.462
$C_{0;i}$	0.610	0.173	0.079	0.011	-0.166
S_i	0.684	0.051	-0.161	-0.469	-1.195

Figure E.3
Tender Offer Firms: Announcement and One to Six Month
Subsequent Indicators
(See Table 6.8, Panel A)

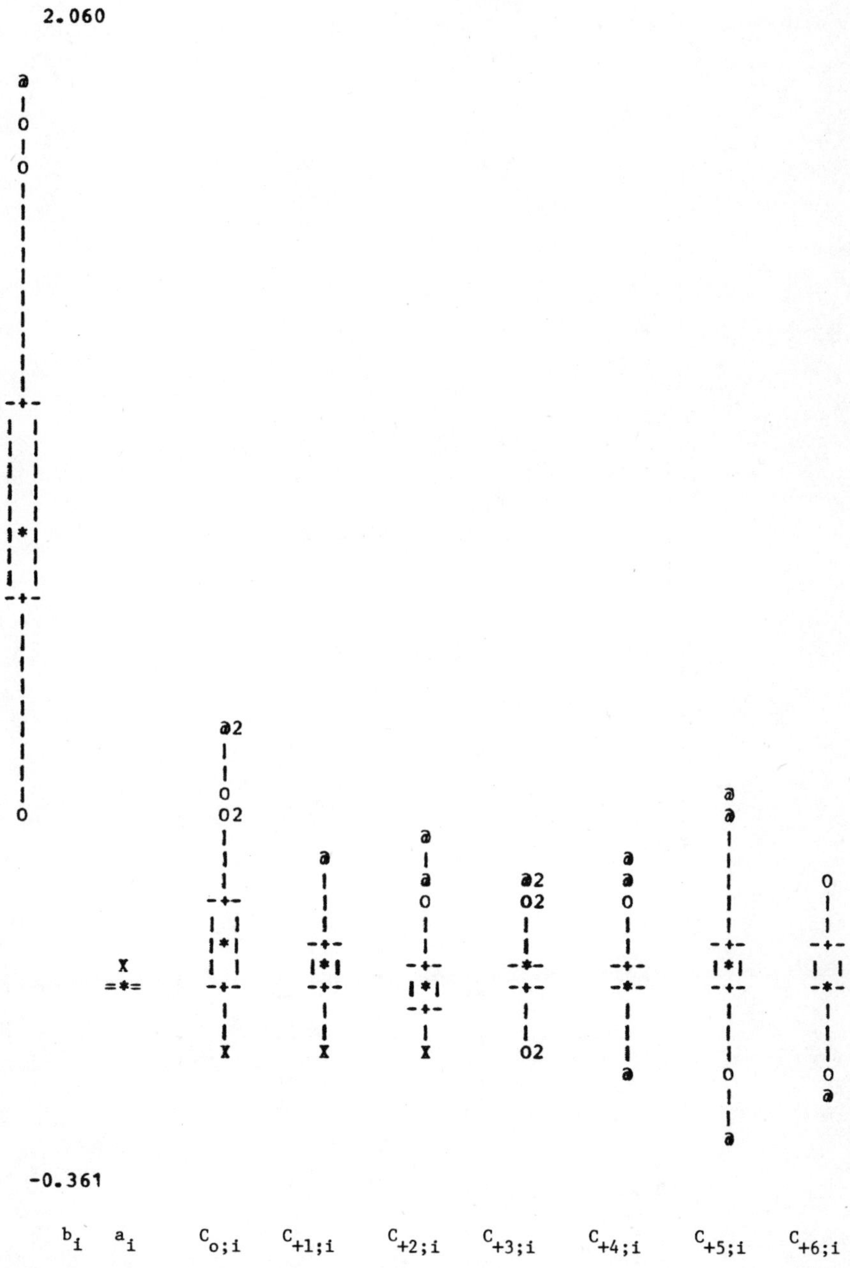

2.060

-0.361

b_i a_i $C_{o;i}$ $C_{+1;i}$ $C_{+2;i}$ $C_{+3;i}$ $C_{+4;i}$ $C_{+5;i}$ $C_{+6;i}$

Figure E.4
Tender Offer Firms: Significant Variables
From Previous Analysis Plus Three Prior Month Indicators
(See Table 6.8, Panel B)

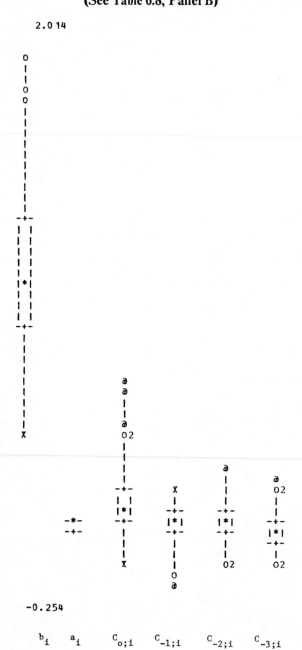

$b_i \qquad a_i \qquad c_{o;i} \qquad c_{-1;i} \qquad c_{-2;i} \qquad c_{-3;i}$

Figure E.5
Tender Offer Firms: Final Model
(See Table 6.8, Panel C)

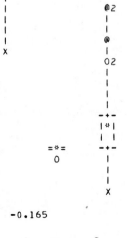

2.027

-0.165

b_i a_i $c_{o;i}$

Appendix E

Figure E.6
Tender Offer Firms: Change in Beta
(See Table 6.9, Panel B)

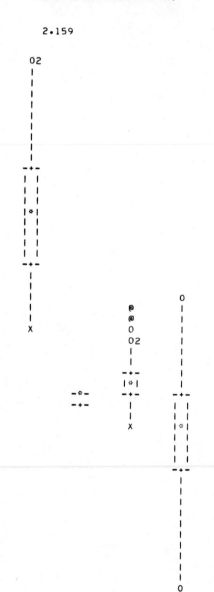

b_i a_i $c_{o;i}$ s_i

Appendix F

Firms Included in Repurchase Study

This appendix describes the firms in the repurchase study of Chapter 6. The information presented here includes:

Cusip Number	for firm identification
Firm Name	
Starting Date	is the month and year 107 months before the first repurchase for each firm
Final Date	is the month and year 60 months subsequent to each firm's last repurchase (or December 1977 which was the last date available on the CRSP tape)
Number of Monthly Returns Available	We attempted to obtain return data on each firm for the time period from the STARTING DATE to the FINAL DATE. This was not always possible, however. In some cases the starting date was before a firm was listed on the CRSP tape. Also, some firms stopped listing before the final date. For this reason another item is included to indicate the total number of monthly returns available for use in the study.
Type(s) of Repurchase	Indicates whether the firm repurchased by tender offer (T) or open market repurchase (O).

Cusip	Firm Name	Starting Date	Final Date	Number of Monthly Returns Available	Type(s) of Repurchase
202410	APL Corporation	3/65	12/77	95	T,T
208010	ATO Inc.	11/63	10/77	120	T
1964510	Allis Chalmers Corporation	3/61	2/75	168	0
2510510	American Chain & Cable Inc.	7/61	6/75	168	0
2532110	American Cyanamid Co.	9/60	6/75	178	0,0
2946510	American Seating Co.	2/62	1/76	168	0
2971710	American Standard, Inc.	10/54	9/68	168	T
3203710	Ampco Pittsburgh Corporation	6/64	12/77	163	T
3948310	Archer Daniels Midland Co.	7/60	6/74	168	0
7323910	Bayuk Cigars, Inc.	7/61	6/75	168	0
9738310	Boise Cascade Corporation	12/64	12/77	150	T
9972510	Borg Warner Corporation	3/61	2/75	168	T
10209710	Bourns, Inc.	5/62	12/77	99	0,0,0
11522310	Brown & Sharpe Manufacturing Co.	2/61	1/75	110	0
11565710	Brown Group Inc.	11/54	10/68	166	T
11704310	Brunswick Corporation	11/63	10/77	168	T
11900710	Budget Inds. Inc.	5/64	12/77	162	0
12065530	Bunker Ramo Corporation	7/64	12/77	114	0
12738810	Cadence Inds. Corporation	4/65	12/77	153	0
13442910	Campbell Soup Co.	8/58	8/75	205	0,0
14233910	Carlisle Corporation	8/61	5/77	190	0,0
14428510	Carpenter Technology Corporation	7/60	7/75	181	0,0
15682510	Cerro Corporation	10/64	12/77	136	T
16326710	Chelsea Inds. Inc.	2/65	12/77	90	T
16789810	Chicago Pneumatic Tool Inc.	6/61	5/75	168	0
17303610	Cities Service Co.	8/60	10/76	195	T,0,0
17859410	City Products Corporation	3/54	2/68	142	T
18600010	Cleveland Cliffs Iron Co.	2/61	1/75	168	0
19605410	Colonial Stores Inc.	12/64	12/77	80	T
20681310	Cone Mls. Corporation	12/61	11/75	168	T
20699090	Conde Nast Publications, Inc.	11/55	10/69	121	T
21181310	Continental Oil Co.	1/63	12/76	168	0
21866110	Cordura Corporation	6/65	12/77	78	T
22439910	Crane Co.	6/50	5/64	168	T
22825510	Crown Cork & Seal Inc.	7/63	6/77	168	0
23156110	Curtiss Wright Corporation	2/57	1/71	168	T
23216510	Cutler Hammer Inc.	12/62	11/76	168	0
23281310	Cyprus Mines Corporation	4/60	12/76	133	0,0
24419910	Deere & Co.	6/60	5/74	168	0
24902810	Dentsply International Inc.	3/61	2/75	168	0
25266910	Diamond International Corporation	5/61	4/75	168	0
26054310	Dow Chemical Co.	12/65	12/77	145	0
26159710	Dresser Industries Inc.	7/56	6/70	168	T
26353410	Du Pont E.I. De Nemours & Co.	9/60	7/77	203	0,T
27646110	Eastern Gas & Fuel Association	8/53	12/77	249	T,T,0

29665910	Esquire Inc.	8/64	12/77	115	0
30726110	Fansteel Inc.	10/63	9/77	151	T
31322510	Federal Co.	10/63	9/77	87	T
31354910	Federal Mogul Corporation	3/61	2/75	168	0
33576510	First National Stores Inc.	9/60	8/74	161	T
36102810	Fuqua Inds. Inc.	8/64	12/77	161	T
36157810	GDV Inc.	2/65	12/77	132	T
36464010	Gamble Skogmo Inc.	1/64	12/77	168	T
37006410	General Host Corporation	1/62	12/75	168	T
37083810	General Signal Corporation	10/60	9/74	168	0
37737010	Glen Alden Corporation	11/62	10/76	120	T
3865320	Grand Un. Co.	7/60	6/74	168	T
39802810	Greyhound Corporation	1/62	12/75	168	0
40018110	Grumman Corporation	3/61	2/75	168	0
40206410	Gulf & Western Inds. Inc.	9/65	12/77	148	T
40246010	Gulf Oil Corporation	3/64	12/77	166	T
40278410	Gulton Inds. Inc.	5/61	4/75	102	0
41030610	Handy & Harman	2/63	1/77	116	0
42343410	Helme Products, Inc.	9/62	8/76	154	0
42705610	Hercules Inc.	6/59	3/74	178	0,0
43609210	Holly Sugar Corporation	5/59	4/73	168	0
44106110	Hospital Affiliates Intl. Inc.	12/65	12/77	66	T
44148810	Houdaille Inds. Inc.	11/53	10/67	168	T
45870210	Interlake Inc.	6/55	8/77	267	T,0
48663810	Kayser Roth Corporation	4/65	12/77	126	T
48724210	Keebler Co.	3/60	2/75	169	0,0
50060210	Koppers, Inc.	2/59	5/73	172	0,0
50075510	Kraft Inc.	10/63	9/77	168	0
52485810	Lehigh Portland Cement Co.	9/59	12/77	217	T,0
52605710	Lennar Corporation	6/64	12/77	65	0
53802110	Litton Industries Inc.	3/57	2/71	163	0
55479010	MacMillan Inc.	2/64	12/77	167	T
56124610	Mallory P.R. & Co., Inc.	1/63	12/76	168	0
57327510	Martin Marietta Corporation	5/56	4/70	168	T
57986510	McCrory Corporation	4/60	3/74	168	T
58016910	McDonnel Douglas Corporation	3/61	2/75	168	0
58062810	McGraw Edison Corporation	1/60	10/74	178	0,0
58256210	McNeil Corporation	7/61	9/77	192	0,T
59160510	Metro Goldwyn Mayer Inc.	6/65	12/77	149	T
59771510	Midland Ross Corporation	11/53	10/67	168	T
60705910	Mobil Corporation	6/59	1/75	188	0,0
60976210	Monogram Ind. Inc. Del.	5/64	12/77	123	T
62664310	Murphy G.C. Co.	8/62	7/76	168	0
62944910	NVF Co.	6/65	12/77	151	T
63512810	National Can Corporation	4/58	3/72	168	T
63565510	National Distillers & Chemical Corp.	3/59	12/77	226	T,0,0
63648610	Naional Inds. Inc.	6/65	12/77	151	T,T
63809710	National Tea Co.	9/57	8/71	168	T
64074510	Neptune Intl. Corporation	1/66	12/77	144	0
65638910	Norris Inds. Inc.	4/64	12/77	165	0
66752810	Northwest Inds. Inc.	4/65	12/77	153	T,T

69076810	Owens Ill. Inc.	2/60	12/77	215	T,0,0
70254410	Pasco Inc.	8/64	12/77	143	T
71602610	Peter Paul Inc.	9/60	7/76	102	0.0
71726510	Phelps Dodge Corporation	7/61	6/75	168	0
73620210	Portec Inc.	4/63	3/77	166	0
74638410	Purolator Inc.	9/61	8/75	148	0
74836910	Questor Corporation	2/65	12/77	153	T
75458610	Raybestos Manhattan Inc.	2/59	1/73	166	0
75946610	Reliance Group Inc.	10/64	12/77	103	T,T
78354910	Ryder Systems Inc.	11/56	10/70	121	T
80370110	Sargent Welch Scientific Co.	8/65	12/77	149	T
80650010	Schenley Inds. Inc.	2/56	1/70	168	T
80974110	Scott Foresman & Co. Del.	1/61	12/74	126	0
81186210	Seagrave Corporation	9/64	12/77	160	0
82662210	Signal Cos. Inc.	7/65	12/77	113	T
82867510	Simmonds Precision Products Inc.	8/64	12/77	111	T
83057510	Skelly Oil Co.	9/54	8/68	168	T
83408610	Sola Basic Inds. Inc.	8/60	7/74	168	T
84723510	Sparton Corporation	8/61	7/75	168	0
84833810	Sperry & Hutchinson Co.	8/60	10/74	99	0,0
86157210	Stone & Webster Inc.	3/62	2/76	168	0
86386310	Studebaker Worthington Inc.	11/60	4/77	113	T,T
86447310	Suburban Propane Gas Corporation	4/60	3/74	160	0
86732310	Sundstrand Corporation	3/60	2/74	168	0
86827310	Superior Oil Co.	5/60	4/75	180	0,0
86971610	Swank Inc.	6/63	5/77	121	0
87264910	TRW Inc.	4/55	3/69	168	T
87538210	Tandy Corporation	5/65	12/77	152	T
87604310	Tappan Co.	12/63	11/77	99	0
88320310	Textron Inc.	7/52	6/66	168	T
90122110	Twentieth Century Fox Film Corp.	4/65	12/77	153	T
90287810	UMC Inds. Inc.	12/61	11/75	168	0
91067110	United Indl. Corporation	1/61	12/74	120	T
91335310	Univar Corporation	7/65	12/77	105	T
92220410	Varian Assoc. Inc.	3/63	2/77	168	0
92242510	Veeder Inds. Inc.	3/59	11/76	129	0,0
92904110	Vornado, Inc.	3/61	2/75	157	0
93443610	Warner Communications Inc.	5/64	12/77	164	0
93444210	Warner Co.	2/59	2/74	178	0,0
94014410	Washington Stl. Corporation	5/63	4/77	110	0
96332010	Whirlpool Corporation	10/53	9/67	152	T
98088110	Woolworth FW Co.	2/59	1/73	168	0
98907010	Zapata Corporation	10/64	12/77	116	T,T

Notes

Chapter 2

1. This theory will be discussed in more detail in Chapter 6.

2. This work is extended in Nantell and Finnerty (1978), a paper submitted to the *Journal of Finance*.

3. Unless otherwise noted, efficiency is used in reference to an asymptotic (large sample) property of the estimators involved. Small sample behavior will be discussed later.

4. We could also allow for differences in the intercept from one time period to the next by introducing dummy variables such as

$$Z_{it} = \begin{cases} 1 \text{ for time period t} \\ 0 \text{ otherwise} \end{cases}$$

   $t = 2, \ldots, T.$

5. As in the covariance model we can also specify a time varying random component, v_t, and write the error components model as

$$R_{it} = a + \sum_{k=1}^{K-1} b_k X_{itk} + w_{it}$$

   where $w_{it} = c_i + v_t + e_{it}$.

   (See Wallace and Hussain (1969), Nerlove (1971b) and Maddala (1971)).

6. The 'mixed model' is simply the RCR model with certain of the coefficient variances constrained to be zero. The separate distinction is made since its use in the literature is minimal. Also, this form of the RCR model will be the basis for the construction of several hypothesis tests in later chapters.

Chapter 3

1. For a definition of convergence in probability see Theil (1971, p. 359) or Rao (1973, p. 110). Convergence in probability is defined as T, the time series length, increases to infinity ($T \to \infty$). Thus, large sample results refer to time series length rather than to the number of cross-sectional units, N.

2. We note without proof that this test can be applied not only to the means of random coefficients but to fixed coefficients as well. In fact, if all coefficients included in the test are fixed, equation (3.31) reduces to the F-ratio for testing

$H_0: \underline{b} = \underline{b}_0$ in a model with a very special type of heteroscedasticity (see Swamy, 1971, pp. 124-26 or, for a more general presentation, Rao, 1973, pp. 188, 196-97). The proof in the case when both fixed and random coefficients are included in the test clearly follows if we view the fixed coefficients as random with variances that are very small. For computational purposes we assign the variances and covariances of these coefficients a value of zero.

3. This was also the case in the full vector test in Appendix C.

4. The test statistic in this form is often referred to as the Chow test for coefficient equality due to an article by Chow (1960) demonstrating its derivation and use.

5. The simplification is achieved by expanding $-2 \ln\lambda$ into an infinite series and dropping those terms which tend to zero as the number of observations tends to infinity. Simplication of the F-statistic in (3.38) will lead to a similar result.

6. The t-statistic can be used to test whether the coefficient is equal to some non-zero value also. We restrict our examination to the "zero case" since it is often used to test whether a particular variable adds significantly to the explanatory power of the regression model.

7. Note the change in degrees of freedom due to the asymptotic theory involved. Also note that t_R is a special case of the F-statistic developed in the previous section. We can test the hypothesis $H_0 : \bar{b} = 0$ using either t_R or $F_R = t_R^2$ where F_R has the F-distribution (asymptotically) with 1 and $N-1$ degrees of freedom.

8. Our t-statistic had 39 degrees of freedom so the standard normal deviate for a 99% confidence interval, 2.58, was used.

9. The result of our argument will follow even if $V\hat{a}r\ (b_i) + V(\hat{b}_i) < 0$ for all j. It is possible, however, for the inequality in step (4) to be reversed if $V\hat{a}r\ (\hat{b}_i) + V(b_i) < 0$ for only some j.

Chapter 4

1. Simultaneous inference is discussed extensively in statistical literature. (See, for example, Miller, 1966).

2. See Appendix C, equation (C.29) and Chapter 3, pages 35–39.

3. The statistic RE is an extension of the statistic developed in Chapter 3 for testing whether coefficients in a pooled model are simultaneously equal to zero.

4. As Johnston (1972, pp. 303-7) points out, if the u_{it}'s are normally and independently distributed, least squares applied to (4.24) will yield consistent estimates of the p_i. The presence of the lagged variables as explanatory variables will cause no problems in terms of large sample properties.

In small samples we know the $\hat{p}_i$ will be biased. The bias is given by

$$E(\hat{p}_i) - p_i \cong -2p_i/T + 0(T^{-1})$$

where $0(T^{-1})$ indicates terms of order less than T^{-1}.

Chapter 5

1. For two statistics to be asymptotically equivalent we mean that their distributions will be the same as the sample size tends to infinity. Thus saying that $(df(R) - df(F)) \cdot F$ and C are symptotically equivalent means that, in the limit, they will have the same distribution. When sample sizes are large, therefore, the choice of one or the other of our test statistics should be of little consequence. Throughout this chapter when we speak of large sample results of asymptotic results we are referring to the time series length, T, and not the number of cross-sectional units, N.

2. $\text{MSE}(\hat{\Theta}) = \text{VAR}(\hat{\Theta}) + (\text{B1AS}(\hat{\Theta}))^2$

3. One problem encountered with this approach is that the RCR program used does not calculate exact MLE's. The estimates from the program are asymptotically equivalent and, thus, the estimated likelihood function will be useful only in large samples. The simulation results reported in Appendix D indicate some of the problems encountered when using these approximate likelihoods from the RCR model. The analytic results of the Box-Cox extension will not be reported at this time. When more exact maximum likelihood techniques are available this result should prove useful in testing for functional form in the RCR model.

4. When predicting a single drawing on the dependent variable for a unit not included in our original sample, the variance of the forecast error becomes much more complex than the term in (5.8). Hocking's results do not provide us with explicit rules in this case on how to increase the precision of our forecasts. Until further research provides guidelines we cannot be sure that deletion of variables will not cause a decrease in precision.

5. These tests are developed under the assumption that the time series length, T, is approaching infinity ($T \rightarrow \infty$). Thus, the best performance of the tests can be expected in samples where T is very large. Since little is known of the small sample properties of these tests, the researcher must recognize the limitations of their use when T is small.

6. We can also test $H_0 : \overline{\underline{b}} = \overline{\underline{b}}_0$ where $\overline{\underline{b}}_0$ is some preassigned vector of values (not necessarily zeros). The test with $\overline{\underline{b}}_0 = 0$ is the test most often seen in practice, however.

Chapter 6

1. As pointed out by several authors, including Stewart (1976) and Marks (1976), there are shortcomings to the methodology used in this study.

2. In the present study all firms examined announced their intention to repurchase stock. Thus we can talk about repurchase *announcement* effects with respect to both tender offer and open market repurchases.

3. The view that security prices appear to reasonably reflect all available information and adjust quickly to new information is well supported. A review of the research in the area of efficient capital markets can be found in Fama (1970).

4. For a detailed valuation model which includes various positive and negative influences discussed previously, see Nantell and Finnerty (1978). They also present a more detailed discussion of the theoretical arguments concerning the direction of the various effects.

5. See Appendix A for a description and critique of the residual analysis methodology.

6. As in Chapter 2

$$R_{it} = \frac{P_{it} - P_{i,t-1} + D_{it}}{P_{i,t-1}}$$

where

P_{it} = price of security i in time period t;
D_{it} = any dividend paid in time period t;
$P_{i,t-1}$ = price of security i in time period t-1;
R_{mt} = Fisher's investment performance index.

7. In studies comparing results from the alternative forms of the market model in (6.1) and (6.2) we usually find little difference in the conclusions.

8. Appendix F lists all firms used in the study as well as the time period for each firm when returns were available.

9. This study is concerned with how the market responds to a repurchase announcement, now how quickly the market responds. Thus, monthly data is appropriate for our purposes. Authors who use daily data (Dann, 1978 for example) are usually concerned with speed of adjustment to new information (market efficiency).

10. See *Federal Reserve Bulletin*, Table 1.10: Monetary Aggregates and Interest Rates.

11. See Chapter 3, Equations (3.45) and (3.46).

12. See Chapter 3, Equation (3.13).

13. See Chapter 3, Equation (3.43).

14. The critical value for the test can be approximated using a formula provided by Burstein (1973). This formula allows the approximation, with very small error, of chi-square percentage points which have not been tabled. The formula will be used throughout the remainder of this chapter, although we will not reference the Burstein article again.

15. The presence of negative serial correlation indicated by our test might be viewed somewhat suspiciously by proponents of the efficient market hypothesis despite some evidence supporting this result. For example, see Fama, et al. (1969) and Schwartz, R.A. and Whitcomb, D.K. (1977), "Evidence on the Presence and Causes of Serial Correlation in Market Model Residuals," *Journal of Financial and Quantitative Analysis*, June, pp. 291-313.

Our RCR results after differencing to remove correlation show little or no change in parameter estimates or the reliability of these estimates. This would seem to indicate that serial correlation of residuals is a minor problem in RCR analyses using the market model. Alternatively, our results could be viewed as an indication that the test for serial correlation developed for pooled data is not performing as well as we might have hoped. Since our test results are consistent with those of previous studies of residual autocorrelation, we will accept the former conclusion. Simulation studies would prove useful in examining the effect of autocorrelated residuals on RCR parameter estimates and inferences.

Programming problems led to the exclusion of the Chapter 4 test for contemporaneous correlation from our analysis. It is hoped that further refinement of this test will be possible in the future.

16. The critical t- and F-statistics values for degrees of freedom not found in tables were approximated using formulae found in Mood, Graybill and Boes (1974, pp. 548-50). The formulae are used throughout the remainder of this chapter although we will not reference Mood, et al. again.

17. We cannot include all the variables of equation (6.4) in our model due to limitations in our RCR computer program. Thus, we will first examine subsequent month effects, then the prior month effects as will be seen in the presentation of results.

18. For a further graphical examination of our results see Appendix E. In this appendix the behavior of the initial OLS estimates of coefficients is examined through the use of boxplots and simple descriptive statistics.

19. Swamy's RCR method involves a two step procedure in which the first step is to estimate a time series regression for each individual. If we attempt to use explanatory variables describing each individual which exhibit cross-section variability but are fixed for each individual over time, our first step in the RCR procedure cannot be completed. The problem is to generalize the procedure to accomodate these purely cross-sectional variables.

Appendix A

1. This is a very general presentation of the methodology. Adjustments are sometimes made to the R_{it} before calculation of residuals. Also, non-parametric tests may be used in lieu of the t-statistic to determine whether effects are significant. This appendix should give a general idea of the nature of the methodology, however.

2. This second stage regression actually needs to be forced through the origin if the residual, e_{it}, and the slope coefficient estimate from the second stage regression are to be equal. However, the argument that follows still holds if a constant term is included in the second stage regression.

3. We should note here that the difference between the estimate of the dummy variable coefficient and the residual may be very small. As Draper and Smith point out, the magnitude of this difference depends on the magnitude of the correlation between the (0,1) dummy variable and our measure of return on the

market, R_{mt}. In other words, if repurchasing stock is correlated with movements in market return we will find larger differences between the two measures of announcement effect. For example, this would occur if firms tend to increase repurchasing activity during a time period when the market is not performing well. There may be some justification for such an hypothesis but we expect the correlation between our two explanatory variables would remain small. Also, if in the first stage regression the announcement month is deleted, then the stagewise approach will produce the same estimate as the multiple regression of R_{it} on R_{mt} and the (0,1) dummy variable.

4. We have thus abandoned stagewise regression for the least squares solution.

5. See Bass (1975) for an alternative approach.

Appendix C

1. This test is discussed extensively in Section II of Chapter 3 of this study.

2. Exact ML estimates are not used due to the extremely complicated system of non-linear equations which would have to be solved in order to obtain these estimates.

Appendix D

1. Only one time series length was examined in this simulation: $T = 50$. The results of such an experiment may be altered by examining series of different lengths. We might, for example, find that the LR equivalent test performs better in larger samples. The length of 50 was an arbitrary choice to aid in deciding which of the tests performs better in a finite but reasonably large sample.

Selected Bibliography

Amemiya, Takeshi (1971). "The Estimation of the Variances in a Variance-Components Model." *International Economic Review,* February, pp. 1–13.

Anderson, T.W. (1958). *An Introduction to Multivariate Statistical Analysis.* New York: John Wiley and Sons, Inc.

Arora, Swarnjit, S. (1973). "Error Components Regression Models and their Applications." *Annuals of Economic and Social Measurement,* Vol. 2, No. 4, pp. 451–61.

Avery, Robert B. (1977). "Error Components and Seemingly Unrelated Regressions." *Econometrica.* January, pp. 199–209.

Balestra, Pietro and Nerlove, Marc. (1966). "Pooling Cross Section and Time Series Data in the Estimation of a Dymanic Model: The Demand for Natural Gas." *Econometrica,* July, pp. 585–612.

Ball, Ray and Brown, Philip. (1968). "An Empirical Evaluation of Accounting Income Numbers." *Journal of Accounting Research,* Autumn, pp. 159–77.

Bass, F.M. and Wittink, D.R. (1975). "Pooling Issues and Methods in Regression Analysis with Examples in Marketing Research." *Journal of Marketing Research,* November, pp. 414–25.

Bierman, H., Jr. and West, R. (1966). "The Acquisition of Common Stock by the Corporate Issuer." *Journal of Finance,* December, pp. 687–96.

Black, Fisher; Jensen, Michael; and Scholes, Myron. (1972). "The Capital Asset Pricing Model: Some Empirical Tests," in M.C. Jensen (ed.), *Studies in the Theory of Capital Markets.* New York: Praeger Publishers.

Boot, John C.G. and Frankfurter, George M. (1972). "The Dynamics of Corporate Debt Management, Decision Rules, and Some Empirical Evidence." *Journal of Financial and Quantitative Analysis,* September, pp. 1957–65.

Box, G.E.P. and Cox, D.R. (1964). "An Analysis of Transformations." *Journal of the Royal Statistical Society Series B* (26), pp. 211–43.

Brownlee, K.A. (1965). *Statistical Theory and Methodology in Science and Engineering.* New York: John Wiley and Sons, Inc.

Burstein, Herman. (1973). "Close Approximation of Percentage Points of the Chi-Square Distribution and Poisson Confidence Limits." *Journal of the American Statistical Association,* September, pp. 581–84.

Chang, Hui-shyong and Lee, Cheng F. (1977). "Using Pooled Time Series and Cross-Section Data to Test the Firm and Time Effects in Financial Analyses." *Journal of Financial and Quantitative Analysis,* September, pp. 457–71.

Chow, Gregory C. (1960). "Tests of Equality Between Sets of Coefficients in Two Linear Regressions." *Econometrica,* July, pp. 591–605.

Cootner, P.H. (1964). *The Random Character of Stock Market Prices.* Cambridge, Mass.: MIT Press.

Dann, Larry Y. (1978). "The Effects of Common Stock Repurchase on Returns to Common Stockholders." Unpublished manuscript presented at Western Economic Association Conference, June.

Dielman, Terry and Wright, Roger. (1977). "Pooling Cross Sectional and Time Series Data – A Review of Statistical Estimation Techniques." University of Michigan Working Paper No. 141, January.

Draper, N.R. and Smith, H. (1966). *Applied Regression Analysis.* New York: John Wiley and Sons, Inc.

Elementary Statistics Using MIDAS.   (1976).   Statistical Research Laboratory, The
   University of Michigan, December, pp. 253–77.

Ellis, Charles and Young, Allan.   (1971).   *The Repurchase of Common Stock.*   New
   York: The Ronald Press Company.

Elton, Edwin and Gruber, Martin.   (1968).   "The Effect of Share Repurchase on the
   Value of the Firm."   *Journal of Finance*, March, pp. 135–49.

Fama, Eugene F.   (1965).   "The Behavior of Stock Market Prices."   *Journal of Business*,
   January, pp. 34–105.

_____.   (1970).   "Efficient Capital Markets: A Review of Theory and Empirical
   Work."   *Journal of Finance*, May, pp. 383–417.

_____;   Fisher, Lawrence; Jensen, Michael C.; and Roll, Richard.   (1969).   "The
   Adjustment of Stock Prices to New Information."   *International Economic Review*,
   February, pp. 1–21.

_____.   and Miller, M.H.   (1972).   *The Theory of Finance.*   New York: Holt,
   Rinehart, and Winston, Inc.

Feige, Edgar and Swamy, P.A.V.B.   (1974).   "A Random Coefficient Model of the
   Demand for Liquid Assets."   *Journal of Money, Credit and Banking*, May, pp.
   241–52.

Finnerty, Joseph E.   (1976).   "Insider's Activity and Inside Information: A Multivariate
   Analysis."   *Journal of Financial and Quantitative Analysis*, June, pp. 205–16.

_____.,   (1976).   "Insider's and Market Efficiency."   *Journal of Finance*, September,
   pp. 1141–49.

Goodnight, James H. and Wallace, T.D.   (1972).   "Operational Techniques and Tables
   for Making Weak MSE Tests for Restrictions in Regressions."   *Econometrica*, July,
   pp. 699–709.

Granger, C.W.J. and Orr, D.   (1972).   "Infinite Variance and Research Strategy in Time
   Series Analysis."   *Journal of the American Statistical Association*, June, pp. 275–85.

Graybill, Franklin A.   (1961).   *Introduction to Linear Statistical Models, Vol. I.*   New
   York: McGraw-Hill Book Company, Inc.

Griffiths, W.E.   (1974).   "Combining Time Series – Cross Section Data: Alternative
   Models and Estimators."   Paper presented at the Fourth Conference of Economists,
   Canberra, August.

Guilkey, D.K. and Schmidt, P.   (1973).   "Estimation of Seemingly Unrelated Regressions
   with Vector Autoregressive Errors."   *Journal of the American Statistical Association*,
   September, pp. 642–47.

Guthart, Leo A.   (1965).   "More Companies Are Buying Back their Stock."   *Harvard
   Business Review*, March-April, pp. 40–45.

Haugen, Robert and Senbet, Lemma.   (1978).   "The Insignificance of Bankruptcy Costs
   to the Theory of Optimal Capital Structure."   *Journal of Finance*, May, pp. 383–94.

Hildreth, Clifford and Houck, James P.   (1968).   "Some Estimators for a Linear Model
   with Random Coefficients."   *Journal of the American Statistical Association*, June, pp.
   584–95.

Hill, B.M.   (1965).   "Inference About Variance Components in the One-Way Model."
   Journal of the American Statistical Association, September, pp. 806–25.

Hoch, Irving.   (1962).   "Estimation of Production Function Parameters Combining Time-
   Series and Cross-Section Data."   *Econometrica*, January, pp. 34–53.

Hocking, R.R.   (1976).   "The Analysis of Selection of Variables in Linear Regression."
   Biometrics, March, pp. 1–50.

Hsiao, Cheng.   (1972).   "The Combined Use of Cross-Section and Time-Series Data in
   Econometric Analysis."   Ph.D. dissertation, Stanford University, August.

_____.(1974). "Statistical Inference for a Model with Both Random Cross-Sectional and Time Effects." *International Economic Review*, February, pp. 12–30.

_____.(1975). "Some Estimation Methods for a Random Coefficient Model." *Econometrica*, March, pp. 305–25.

Huang, C.J. and Bolch, B.W. (1974). "On the Testing of Regression Disturbances for Normality." *Journal of the American Statistical Association*, June, pp. 330–35.

Hussain, Ashiq. (1969). "A Mixed Model for Regressions." *Biometrika*, August, pp. 327–36.

Jaffe, Jeffrey F. (1974). "Special Information and Insider Trading." *Journal of Business*, July, pp. 410–28.

Johnson, K.H. and Lyon, H.L. (1973). "Experimental Evidence on Combining Cross-Section and Time Series Information." *The Review of Economics and Statistics*, November, pp. 465–74.

Johnson, J. (1972). *Econometric Methods*. New York: McGraw-Hill Book Co.

Kakwani, N.C. (1967). "The Unbiasedness of Zellner's Seemingly Unrelated Regression Equation Estimators." *Journal of the American Statistical Association*, March, pp. 141–42.

Kendall, Maurice G. and Stuart, Alan. (1969). *The Advanced Theory of Statistics: Volume 1: Distribution Theory*. New York: Hafner Publishing Co.

King, B.F. (1966). "Market and Industry Factors in Stock Price Behavior." *Journal of Business*, January, pp. 139–90.

Kmenta, J. and Gilbert, R.F. (1968). "Small Sample Properties of Alternative Estimators of Seemingly Unrelated Regressions." *Journal of the American Statistical Association*, December, pp. 1180–1200.

_____. and Gilbert R.F. (1970). "Estimation of Seemingly Unrelated Regressions with Autoregressive Disturbances." *Journal of the American Statistical Association*, March, pp. 186–97.

Kmenta, Jan. (1971). *Elements of Econometrics*. New York: Macmillan Publishing Co., Inc.

Kuh, E. (1959). "The Validity of Cross-Sectionally Estimated Behavior Equations in Time Series Applications." *Econometrica*, April, pp. 197–214.

Lilliefors, Hubert W. (1967). "On the Kolmogorov-Smirnov Test for Normality with Mean and Variance Unknown." *Journal of the American Statistical Association*, June, pp. 399–402.

Maddala, G.S. (1971). "The Use of Variance Components Models in Pooling Cross-Section and Time Series Data." *Econometrica*, March, pp. 341–58.

_____. (1977). *Econometrics*. New York: McGraw-Hill Book Co.

_____. and Mount, T.D. (1973). "A Comparative Study of Alternative Estimators for Variance Components Models Used in Econometric Applications." *Journal of the American Statistical Association*, June, pp. 324–28.

Marcis, R.G. and Smith, V.K. (1974). "Efficient Estimation of Multivariate Financial Relationships." *Journal of Finance*, December, pp. 1415–23.

Marks, Kenneth R. (1976). *The Stock Price Performance of Firms Repurchasing Their Own Shares*. New York University Bulletin.

McHugh, R.B. and Mielke, P.W. (1968). "Negative Variance Components and Statistical Dependence in Nested Sampling." *Journal of the American Statistical Association*, September, pp. 1000–3.

McNeil, Donald R. (1977). *Interactive Data Analysis*. New York: John Wiley and Sons.

Miller, R.G., Jr. (1966). *Simultaneous Statistical Inference*. New York: McGraw-Hill Book Company, Inc.

Modigliani, Franco and Pogue, Gerald A. (1974). "An Introduction to Risk and Return." *Financial Analysts Journal*, March-April, pp. 68–86.

Mood, Alexander; Grayhill, Franklin; and Boes, Duane. (1974). *Introduction to the Theory of Statistics.* New York: McGraw-Hill Book Co.

Moriarty, M. (1975). "Cross Sectional, Time Series Issues in the Analysis of Marketing Decision Variables." *Journal of Marketing Research*, May, pp. 142-50.

Mundlak, Yair. (1978). "On the Pooling of Time Series and Cross Section Data." *Econometrica*, January, pp. 69–85.

Nantell, Timothy and Finnerty, Joseph. (1974). "Effect of Stock Repurchases on Price Performance." University of Michigan Working Paper No. 94, October.

_____.and Finnerty, Joseph. (1978). "Effect of Large Tender Offer Repurchases on Stockholder Wealth." Paper submitted to *Journal of Finance*, 1978.

Nerlove, Marc. (1971a). "Further Evidence on the Estimation of Dynamic Economic Relations from a Time Series of Cross-Sections." *Econometrica*, March, pp. 359–82.

_____. (1971b). "A Note on Error Components Models." *Econometrica*, March, pp. 383–96.

Neter, John and Wasserman, William. (1974). *Applied Linear Statistical Models.* Homewood, Illinois: Richard D. Irwin, Inc.

Norgaard, Richard and Corine. (1974). "A Critical Examination of Share Repurchase." *Financial Management*, Spring, pp. 44–51.

Parks, R.W. (1967). "Efficient Estimation of a System of Regression Equations when Disturbances are Both Serially and Contemporaneously Correlated." *Journal of the American Statistical Association*, June, pp. 500–9.

Pearson, E.S.; D'Agostino, R.B.; and Bowman, K.O. (1977). "Tests for Departure from Normality: Comparison of Powers." *Biometrika*, August, pp. 231–46.

Pindyck, Robert S. and Rubinfeld, Daniel L. (1976). *Econometric Models and Economic Forecasts.* New York: McGraw-Hill Book Co.

Porter, R.D. (1973). "On the Use of Sample Survey Weights in the Linear Models." *Annals of Economic & Social Measurement*, April, pp. 141–58.

Rao, C.R. (1973). *Linear Statistical Inference and Its Applications.* New York: John Wiley and Sons.

_____. (1965). "The Theory of Least Squares When the Parameters are Stochastic and its Application to the Analysis of Growth Curves." *Biometrika*, December, pp. 447–58.

_____. (1972). "Estimation of Variance and Covariance Components in Linear Models." *Journal of the American Statistical Association*, March, pp. 112–15.

Revankar, Nagesh S. (1974). "Some Finite Sample Results in the Context of Two Seemingly Unrelated Regression Equations." *Journal of the American Statistical Association*, March, pp. 187–90.

Rosenberg, Barr. (1973a). "A Survey of Stochastic Parameter Regression." *Annals of Economic and Social Measurement*, Vol. 2, No. 4, pp. 381–97.

_____. (1973b). "The Analysis of a Cross Section of Time Series by Stochastically Convergent Parameter Regression." *Annals of Economic and Social Measurement*, Vol. 2, No. 4, pp. 399–428.

_____. (1973c). "Linear Regression with Randomly Dispersed Parameters." *Biometrika*, April, pp. 65–72.

_____. (1974). "Extra-Market Components of Covariance in Security Returns." *Journal of Financial and Quantitative Analysis*, March, pp. 263–74.

_____. and McKibben, Walt. (1973). "The Prediction of Systematic Risk in Common Stocks." *Journal of Financial and Quantitative Analysis*, March, pp. 317–33.

Rosenberg, Marvin and Young, Allan. (1976). "The Performance of Common Stocks Subsequent to Repurchase by Recent Tender Offers." *Quarterly Review of Economics and Business,* Spring, pp. 109–13.

Scheffe, H. (1959). *The Analysis of Variance.* New York: John Wiley and Sons.

Shapiro, S.S. and Francia, R.S. (1972). "Approximate Analysis of Variance Test for Normality." *Journal of the American Statistical Association,* March, pp. 215–16.

_____., Wilk, M.B., and Chen, Mrs. H.J. (1968). "A Comparative Study of Various Tests for Normality." *Journal of the American Statistical Association,* December, pp. 1343–72.

Sharpe, William F. (1963). "A Simplified Model for Portfolio Analysis." *Management Science,* January, pp. 277–93.

Singh, Balvir, and Ullah, Aman. (1974). "Estimation of Seemingly Unrelated Regressions With Random Coefficients." *Journal of the American Statistical Association,* March, 191–95.

Srivastava, V.K. (1970). "The Efficiency of Estimating Seemingly Unrelated Regression Equations." *Annals of the Institute of Statistical Mathematics,* Vol. 22, pp. 483–93.

Stewart, Samuel S. (1976). "Should a Corporation Repurchase its Own Stock?" *The Journal of Finance,* June, pp. 911–21.

Swamy, P.A.V.B. (1970). "Efficient Inference in a Random Coefficient Regression Model." *Econometrica,* March, pp. 311–23.

_____. (1971). Statistical Inference in Random Coefficient Regression Models. Berlin: Springer-Verlag.

_____. (1973). "Criteria Constraints and Multicollinearity in Random Coefficient Regression Models." *Annals of Economic and Social Measurement,* Vol. 2, No. 4, pp. 429–50.

_____. (1974). "Linear Models with Random Coefficients," in *Frontiers in Econometrics,* Paul Zarembka (ed.) New York: Academic Press, Inc.

_____., and Arora, Swarnjit, S. (1972). "The Exact Finite Sample Properties of the Estimators of Coefficients in the Error Components Regression Models." *Econometrica,* March, pp. 261–75.

_____., and Metha, J.S. (1973). "Bayesian Analysis of Error Components Regression Models." *Journal of the American Statistical Association,* September, pp. 648–58.

_____., and Metha, J.S. (1975). "On Bayesian Estimation of Seemingly Unrelated Regressions When Some Observations are Missing." *Journal of Econometrics,* May, pp. 157–69.

_____., and Metha, J.S. (1975). "Bayesian and Non-Bayesian Analysis of Switching Regressions and of Random Coefficient Regression Models." *Journal of the American Statistical Association,* September, pp. 593–602.

_____., and Metha, J.S. (1976). "Further Evidence on the Relative Efficiencies of Zellner's Seemingly Unrelated Regression Estimators." *Journal of the American Statistical Association,* September, pp. 634–39.

_____., and Metha, J.S. (1977). "Estimation of Linear Models with Time and Cross Sectionally Varying Coefficients." *Journal of the American Statistical Association,* December, pp. 890–98.

Theil, Henri. (1971). *Principles of Econometrics.* New York: John Wiley and Sons, Inc.

Tiao, G.C., and Tan, W.Y. (1965). "Bayesian Analysis of Random-Effect Models in the Analysis of Variance. I. Posterior Distribution of Variance-Components." *Biometrika,* June, pp. 37–53.

_____., and Tan, W.Y. (1966). "Bayesian Analysis of Random-Effect Models in the Analysis of Variance. II. Effect of Autocorrelated Errors." *Biometrika*, December, pp. 477–95.

Toro-Vizcarrondo, Carlos, and Wallace, T.D. (1968). "A Test of the Mean Square Error Criterion for Restrictions in Linear Regression." *Journal of the American Statistical Association*, June, pp. 558–72.

Wallace, T.D. (1972). "Weaker Criteria and Tests for Linear Restrictions in Regression." *Econometrica*, July, pp. 689–98.

_____., and Hussain, A. (1969). "The Use of Error Components Models in Combining Cross-Section with Time Series Data." *Econometrica*, January, pp. 55–72.

_____., and Toro-Vizcarrondo, Carlos, (1969). "Tables for the Mean Square Error Test for Exact Linear Restrictions in Regressions." *Journal of the American Statistical Association*, December, pp. 1649–63.

Wright, Roger; Dielman, Terry; and Nantell, Timothy. (1977a). "Analysis of Stock Repurchases with a Random Coefficient Regression Model." (University of Michigan Working Paper #149): Journal of the American Statistical Association Business and Economic Proceedings, *Chicago, Illinois, pp. 345–48.*

_____., Nantell, Timothy; and Dielman, Terry. (1977b). "Interactive Statistical Analysis of a Cross-Section of Multivariate Time Series with an Application in Financial Analysis." Midwest AIDS proceedings, Cleveland, Ohio.

Young, Allan. (1967). "The Performance of Common Stocks Subsequent to Repurchase." *Financial Analysts Journal*, September-October, pp. 117–21.

_____., and Marshall, Wayne. (1971). "Controlling Shareholder Servicing Costs." *Harvard Business Review*, January/February, pp. 71–78.

Zellner, Arnold. (1962). "An Efficient Method of Estimating Seemingly Unrelated Regressions and Tests for Aggregation Bias." *Journal of the American Statistical Association*, June, pp. 348–68.

_____. (1963). "Estimators for Seemingly Unrelated Regression Equations: Some Exact Finite Sample Results." *Journal of the American Statistical Association*, December, pp. 977–92.

_____., and Huang, David S. (1962). "Further Properties of Efficient Estimators for Seemingly Unrelated Regressions." *International Economic Review*, pp. 300–313.

Index